"John Baylor Prep is about helping our students achieve the American Dream. In [...] will learn about the simple steps [...] igh school students the best oppor [...] ohn Baylor does a great job of hel [...] navigate the academic and financial world of college. *Reaching Higher* is helping our kids grow their opportunities for success!"

—James Sutfin, Superintendent
Millard Public Schools

"Being able to help high schoolers improve ACT scores and make sound decisions about college is a cornerstone of being a good high school administrator. John Baylor's book is a powerful tool we are using as a staff at Bennington to proactively guide both students and parents toward preparing for college. I wish I'd have had the book 10 years ago when I started as a principal."

—Matthew Blomenkamp, Principal
Bennington High School

Dad -
I am so proud of the man you are and will be. We are family. We are here for you whenever. My kids love you and so do Susan and I. Thanks for all your generosity and thoughtfulness (and tasty food!)
Love, Jonathan

10/15/15

REACHING HIGHER

The Simple Strategy to Transform America's K-12 Schools

JOHN BAYLOR

Lincoln, Nebraska

Reaching Higher
The Simple Strategy to Transform America's K-12 Schools

ISBN: 978-1-942412-04-5

Library of Congress Cataloging Number: 2015933557

Publisher Cataloging in Publication Data on file with the publisher.

www.JohnBaylorPrep.com

Publishing and production: Concierge Marketing Inc.

Printed in the USA

10 9 8 7 6 5 4 3 2

This is dedicated to two great teachers, who gave me in
my teens a love for deep thinking and learning, and whose
techniques I use every day:
Mr. (John) Tulp and Mr. (Jim) Beaton.

JBP's Mission:
HELP SCHOOLS AND FAMILIES
CREATE TWO- AND FOUR-YEAR
COLLEGE GRADUATES
WITH MINIMAL DEBT.

CONTENTS

SECTION 2 - HOW?

PREFACE

This book is for K-12 teachers and administrators: our front line. You are teaching in this new educational world of high stakes testing and reformers. Thank you cards and apples have given way to critiques from every direction. Teaching is a tougher, more scrutinized, and more important job than ever. Meanwhile, eighty percent of a student's waking hours during grades Kindergarten through twelve are spent outside of school.[1]

As a motivational speaker and test prep teacher, I have visited hundreds of high schools. No matter how large or small the school, it's often easy to see clumps of disengaged, sometimes hostile students, distracted and uninterested.

A high school principal in a rural school told me, "John, I can't reach these kids anymore. I'm retiring after this year. I'm too old for this."

One of my company's instructors left her full time job as a math teacher at a big, diverse, urban public high school because the students' apathy and disrespect appalled her.

An assistant principal at a high school of twelve hundred students with a 50 percent free and reduced lunch rate told me that about one hundred of her students are truant each day. She also noted that one-third of her sophomore students (eighty five kids) were failing two or more classes with one week left in the first half of second semester.

This book outlines a cure to this apathy that afflicts too many students in our nation's schools. Here is the simple strategy to attack the student disengagement that is undermining not only the educational outcomes of our children, but also the job satisfaction and effectiveness of our educators: a powerful game plan to create motivation and improved results that teachers and administrators can implement immediately, with minimal cost and minimum controversy.

Imagine how much more enjoyable your teaching day would be if it were filled with more enthusiastic students. Imagine disciplining less and teaching more. Imagine parents regularly supporting you, pushing their students to achieve. Most teachers stay in the same school district throughout their career, so you will personally reap the benefits of this plan.

Reaching Higher is intended for educators who want to go on offense for the benefit of their students, their school culture, their academic outcomes, and their own happiness. I hope that you receive its message in that spirit, for I believe there should be no more respected profession than *school teacher*.

SECTION 1 - WHY?

THE CHALLENGE AND
THE STRATEGY TO FIX IT

The class for ninety eleventh graders began at noon. About twenty arrived late. About ten brought lunch, chomping away loudly. Most sauntered lazily toward seats surrounding circular tables in the school cafeteria, their voices smothering mine.

I pulled the microphone closer.

"Why are we here? Why does learning matter? There are a lot of reasons, but here's one. Those of you who get a two- or four-year college degree with minimal debt will have dramatically improved your life's chances. Why? You will soon enter a hypercompetitive, capitalistic, global economy powered by two forces making life really tough for those without two- or four-year college degrees. These two forces will soon be fierce competitors of yours. What are they?" The room began to quiet.

"Intelligent machines and inexpensive foreign workers. Each month, they become more capable, plentiful, and affordable. Skills and knowledge will equip you to compete against and stay ahead of these potent foes rather than succumb to them.

"A two- or four-year college degree with minimal debt is a proven pathway to the skills and knowledge so critical for future success versus these potent competitors—but avoid overspending and overborrowing. Step one is to go to the right college at the right price."

"When determining who gets in and at what cost, colleges care most about the Big Three: Grades, Scores, and One Extracurricular. Try today, become a two- or four-year college graduate with minimal debt by age 24, and then compete with skills and knowledge, free from hefty monthly student loan payments. Students who try harder today should live easier tomorrow."

The cacophony in that cafeteria gave way to silence and eventually rapt attention. Clearly, stating the Mission had worked again. Suddenly armed with context—and a picture of a brighter future—the students intently listened and learned.

I soon gave all ninety an English passage filled with grammar questions and left the room—the only audible sounds coming from scribbling pencils and pens.

We can and we must take back our classrooms, delivering meaningful messages along with curriculum. Doing so involves a simple strategy, a powerful Mission really, that viscerally reaches students and parents. This book shows how simple and transformative this Mission and its ramifications can be.

Let's go on offense, together: teachers, administrators, parents, students, and lawmakers. We can do better.

Bullying, tardiness, truancy, defiance, and distractions are all symptoms of an insidious underlying cause—disengaged, unmotivated students. Educators often resign themselves to the student apathy afflicting their classes and school. However, armed with a simple strategy embracing a simple message and Mission, we can create more motivated students and parents, attacking apathy itself rather than its symptoms.

We need to because the unmotivated student today is likely a struggling adult tomorrow—due to an awaiting hypercompetitive capitalistic world.

I often ask high school teachers, "Are students today easier to teach, harder to teach, or unchanged compared to their predecessors?" The vast majority of hands agree with the research: students today are harder to reach and teach. Students today are simply less motivated than their predecessors.

Slightly more than a decade ago, the 2003 National Research Council Report on Motivation showed that 40 percent of high school students are disengaged.[2] The more recent 2012 Gallup Student Poll declared that 60 percent of students are unmotivated and disconnected.[3]

Let's go on offense, together: teachers, administrators, parents, students, and lawmakers. We can do better.

Bill Gates says, "The one thing we have a lot of in the United States is unmotivated students."[4]

In 2011 a rural high school principal told me that historically about 33 percent of his seniors attended four-year colleges, but that only 9 percent of that year's senior class would attend. Discouraged high school administrators consistently tell me that "Senioritis" is rampant. As the leaves fall each autumn, so too does motivation for too many high school seniors.

A terrific teacher recently returned to his high school to teach after three years in central administration. He said, "Before I left, most students had cell phones. Now, most students have smart phones. They check them constantly, sometimes without even realizing they're doing it. I'll be talking to a student, and she'll keep glancing at her phone—right in front of me, sometimes right after I've asked her to stop. These smart phones mesmerize the kids. It's more and more difficult to reach them."

A few years ago I asked a high school staff, "What percentage of your students do the assigned homework on an average night?" The answer was about 25 percent. Those teachers expected about one of every four students to complete assigned homework on any given night. Someday, those students will learn what their disengagement has cost them—in college success, in career satisfaction, and in their chances for upward mobility.

This message is not just for the poor and underprivileged, because even the college-bound can be void of intrinsic desire to learn. Denise Pope, a Stanford education department researcher, wrote in 2003 about Silicon Valley students in *Doing School: How We Are Creating a Generation of Stressed-Out, Materialistic, and Miseducated Students.* Pushed by demanding parents and expectations, these students did not truly engage in their AP courses and extracurricular activities, instead enduring them primarily to gild their college application credentials.[5] Even our best students are often going through the motions, rarely engaging deeply for the excitement of learning.

Excellent Sheep by former Yale Professor William Deresiewicz is effectively the thematic sequel to *Doing School*, lamenting a similar detachment in today's elite college students. Deresiewicz spends hundreds of pages describing talented students void of passion, simply accumulating accomplishments, caught in a credentials race afflicting too many affluent youth. Deresiewicz claims that the conveyor belt leading to coveted selective college admissions slots has robbed high-achieving adolescents of their passion, depth, and curiosity. He believes that productive passions should be fostered rather than traded for an AP Statistics class that looks better on a transcript, that an inspiring art class should be rewarded in college admissions with the same respect as an honors Spanish class.

Deep engagement in learning for its own sake is rare.

Deresiewicz cites that 21 percent of US college students major in Business, while only 3 percent major in English, illustrating practicality, perhaps, but not passion.[6] Some of those Business majors may truly have passion for those business administration lectures, but logic suggests that it's less than one of every five college students. Deep engagement in learning for its own sake is rare.

The average US citizen watches 28 hours of TV each week, tied for first in the developed world with Great Britain.[7] [8] For every three hours a child in the US is in school, he will watch five hours of television.[9] Of course, there are some truly engaged students that we get to teach every day, but it's the majority that we need to target. Student behavior is one reason why more than 40 percent of K-12 teachers leave the profession within five years.[10]

One simple strategy—a simple, sustained, tested, and proven message—can reach disengaged students and make them want to learn. It's a strategy and message that can transform schools.

ONE SIMPLE STRATEGY

Consider the three possible outcomes for all Kindergarten through twelfth grade students. Each will experience an adulthood armed with one of these:

1. No two- or four-year college degree

2. A two- or four-year college degree with a lot of debt

3. A two- or four-year college degree with minimal to no debt

There may appear to be a fourth option: for-profit trade schools offering training and credentials that seem to fall outside the typical definition of a two-year college degree. These for-profit schools can offer varying durations, costs, and quality. However, leaving aside this niche and often expensive option, there are no other possible outcomes. All of our effort will send nearly every one of our students to one of the three possible destinations listed above.

Most educators, parents, and students prefer #3, especially when fully understanding the alternatives. When I explain all three choices to assembled students, usually 100 percent of the hands commit to #3.

There are families that champion Outcome #3—many of us educators grew up in one. There are heroic teachers regularly banging the college expectation drum so that the unmotivated are outliers. Yet in the average school day filled with important teaching, unplanned distractions, and countless conversations, rarely do schools culturally communicate the three outcomes or promote the preferred one, partially explaining why 60 percent of US adults have neither a two-year nor a four-year college degree[11] and the average amount of debt for a four-year graduate at graduation is $30,000.[12]

Clarifying the destination helps the ship find and stay the course. Failure to clarify can relegate outcomes to chance.

Imagine the motivational impact if your school changed its Mission to "We create two- and four-year college graduates with minimal debt." It's simple but profound.

This book explores the transformative effect this overt, simple *Reaching Higher* Mission can have on students, parents, and staff. It explores how such a clear, concrete, measurable goal improves motivation, morale, engagement, test scores, and all academic results, while providing consistency to policies and purpose. It walks through how to successfully implement and measure this Mission. It explores the objections made by detractors who feel that such a goal isn't inclusive, feasible, or appropriate.

Transformative results and minimal cost are rare companions. But they can be within our schools when we seek to create college graduates with minimal debt. Let's examine why we should.

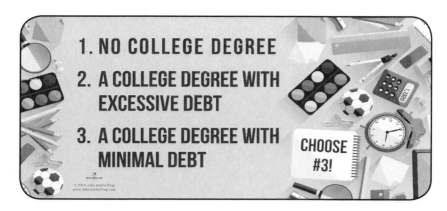

II

TURN YOUR STUDENTS INTO COLLEGE GRADUATES WITH MINIMAL DEBT

Disengagement has multiple victims: the individual, the family, the teachers, the school, and the greater society. School is an economic launching pad. Undeveloped human capital comes at an increasingly high human and social cost because the world has changed. And the rate of change is accelerating; yesterday's average performance will likely be tomorrow's failing grade.

But just how specifically have job expectations changed? Frequently communicating that story to students and parents is critical for motivating them and for going on offense.

You can have more students showing genuine interest and appreciation. You can have more of your students doing the homework. You can inspire students to help you quiet the disruptive knuckleheads. You can create supportive parents, your new allies. Together we can instill stronger extrinsic motivation in our students.

It's important to clarify our purpose. Is it to create life-long learners, character, leadership, self-sufficiency, championship sports teams, higher test scores, higher high school graduation rates, or some composite of multiple goals? I used to think the primary purpose of education was to teach every student how to communicate persuasively—the prerequisite for influence. "We create two- and four-year college graduates with minimal debt" provides clarity, direction, and measurable objectives. It also aligns your school's Mission with the interests of your constituents, whether they know it yet or not. All policies can be compared against and feed into this one overarching Mission.

What do we currently ask schools to prioritize? One educator puts it this way: "All my administrators care about are (our state's) test scores and high school graduation rates." Another administrator admits, "Yes, test scores and high school graduation rates are our end game."

And that's what we ask educators to care about. They're simply following our priorities: test, test, and test the heck out of these kids and get them a high school diploma.

My fourth grader, Antonia, told me last year that she did well on her state tests. I said, "Great." She said, "Well we've been preparing for them for weeks."

Teachers are fed up. A fabulous, engaging teacher recently retired early from my children's elementary school. She told me that she didn't want to spend so much time preparing kids for the tests. She wanted to teach.

All this 'No Child Left Behind'-mandated testing hasn't hurt the national high school graduation rate, which from 2000 to 2015 rose from 72% to 81%.[13] But we should be able to find a happier balance while still increasing high school graduation rates. Although test scores that colleges value do serve the college graduation Mission, the obsession with the latest annual state test scores seems excessive, creating hours of preparation and test taking that drains enthusiasm from students and teachers.

And high school graduation rates also do matter, but not as an ends. Work-place expectations have changed. High school graduation has become a means to the ends, the new goal: a two- or four-year college degree with minimal debt. Measuring high school graduation rates rather than college graduation rates is like believing the score at the end of the third quarter matters more than the score at the end of the game.

Measuring high school graduation rates rather than college graduation rates is like believing the score at the end of the third quarter matters more than the score at the end of the game.

Leaders of elite schools filled with privileged, affluent students don't need to explain why graduating from college matters. The expectation of a college degree already resides in those students' homes. These schools can bypass this part of the Mission and go straight to how to become a college graduate with minimal debt. Even the affluent family now often wants to learn about strategies to avoid a $50,000 annual price tag for college and alternatives to Hobart, University of Virginia, Notre Dame, Columbia, Boston University, and the many other colleges featuring a retail sticker price of more than $50,000 a year.

A two- or four-year college degree with minimal debt should arm students with knowledge, skills, and financial freedom: the tools to upward mobility and self-actualized lives. Put simply, one's life chances improve with a college degree and minimal to no debt.

In January of 2014 I was shopping at my local grocery store. A teenage worker recognized me and introduced herself. I knew her siblings and mother well but little about her, other than she was a twelfth grader and played varsity tennis. And so I asked my normal questions, "What's the plan for college? How many colleges are you waiting to hear from? What's the dream five, ten years from now?"

She said, "I'll probably apply to the local Community College or perhaps Wayne State."

I knew that each of these schools can be an excellent choice at a very reasonable cost. But I knew that neither offered women's tennis."

So I prodded, "Do you hate tennis?"

"No, I love tennis."

"Is there any other passion you're planning on quitting prematurely? Are you planning on attending a college that won't let you eat ice cream?"

She started to laugh, and then she started to tear up.

It was late January, very late in the application process. Many worthy, affordable colleges have application deadlines prior to late January. Her family lived modestly, and she had three siblings. I helped her apply to about nine colleges— each offering rigorous educations, reasonable net costs, and women's tennis.

About two months later, three were bidding for her: Ohio Wesleyan, Earlham, and Knox College. She now plays varsity tennis at Knox College, paying a net cost of about $14,000 a year. She'll annually earn about $5,000 and borrow about $5,000, the maximum I always recommend. Her parents can handle the rest: about $350 a month. She is happy.

Somehow she had never received the Mission that the 'best fit' college requiring minimal debt was the goal. She hadn't heard that an extracurricular skill—if marketed well—can trigger scholarships and dramatically improve the college experience, increasing the likelihood of graduating. But even if she had, her college counselors had not given her the tools to execute the goal. She told me that her few meetings with counselors had primarily consisted of conversations confirming that she was on track to graduate from high school. Though she had received a sound high school education, the school's overall Mission had stopped short rather than aligning with her true interest: a meaningful college experience and a degree with minimal debt.

By focusing solely on Kindergarten through twelfth grade, her school had done everything well, according to that measure. Yet she was on the verge of settling for the wrong college for *her*, undermining thirteen years of significant personal and community effort and cost.

I remember John Baylor Prep's first year helping Marengo (IL) High School's juniors: 2010. I asked many students before class and in the halls, "What's the plan for college? How many colleges are you applying to? What's the dream five, ten years from now?" I often received blank looks, even from seniors. This was not yet a high school with a Mission to create college graduates with minimal debt. These students didn't yet know that the world had changed. Their principal soon urged teachers to regularly ask students similar future-focused questions. In subsequent years, Marengo's students were far more likely to have answers—and much higher test scores as well.

I was teaching grammar recently to a class of twenty-six seniors preparing for the December ACT. It was a Monday, and the deadline for signing up for that ACT was the following Friday. The December ACT is typically the final one considered for financial aid. I asked, "How many of you are signed up for the December ACT?" Three hands went up. These twenty-six seniors were all college-bound, yet only three

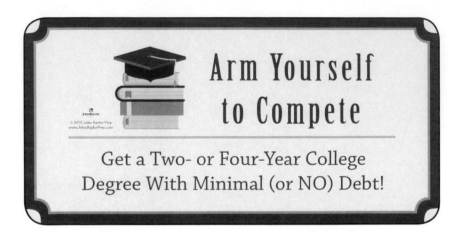

Arm Yourself to Compete

Get a Two- or Four-Year College Degree With Minimal (or NO) Debt!

of them had done the minimal online effort required to sign up for a test that could significantly affect the cost and quality of their future college.

These uninformed scholars came from a high school with 65 percent of its students receiving free and reduced lunch. Amidst such challenges, a central, unifying Mission could have ensured that everyone long since understood the stakes and the steps to improve their futures. If twenty-three of twenty-six seniors preparing for an ACT are about to miss the deadline for signing up for their final, meaningful chance to take the ACT test, presumably those percentages extended across the entire student population. Creating motivated students throughout middle and high school means a clear goal, regularly explaining its relevance, and ensuring everyone knows how to accomplish it.

CREATING A MISSION STATEMENT

Here is a current Mission statement in a school board room. Does it inspire or clarify?

"Our elementary school seeks to create a challenging learning environment that encourages high expectations for success through development-appropriate instruction that allows for individual differences and learning styles. Each student's self-esteem is fostered by positive relationships with students and staff."[14] It goes on.

Good luck finding any benefit from that or most school Mission statements. One reason is that there's rarely any way to measure them against actual results. Perhaps the Mission is being met, but which part and who would know?

Or there's this: "Our school strives to make children confident and creative builders of their future. Our focus is on the whole child. We work toward an integrated curriculum that reaches across disciplines and age levels; the students are encouraged to meet academic challenges with openness, enthusiasm, and a willingness to solve problems."[15]

A typical school Mission statement requires months to finalize and minutes to forget. Such benign, well-meaning Missions are common, though rarely catalysts for motivation or learning.

Clarity, brevity, and measurability *create* messaging power. Less is more. People crave clear, concise expectations. And if the Mission is measurable, it has power and potential.

Dean Smith, legendary North Carolina basketball coach, had a simple credo: "Play hard. Play smart. Play together." When his team measured well in these three areas, it rarely lost. Wins were the natural result of a well-conceived, well-executed Mission.

Starbucks's guiding principle instructs and informs any employee or customer. "Our Mission: to inspire and nurture the human spirit—

A typical school mission statement requires months to finalize and minutes to forget.

one person, one cup, and one neighborhood at a time."[16] Their guiding principle instructs and informs any employee or customer.

Clarity, brevity, and measurability equal messaging power.

Your school's Mission Statement could be this brief, clear, and measurable: "We create two- and four-year college graduates with minimal debt." It can have a powerful cumulative effect on students, parents, teachers, school districts, communities, and states. Excellence, responsibility, character, leadership, success, tolerance, and all the happy nouns and adjectives filling educational Mission Statements usually lack that last attribute—they're not measurable.

Every school district in this country can have the National Clearinghouse quantify the exact percentage of its graduates that attain a two- or four-year college degree within six years. The cost and effort to do so are nominal. This data matters because a college degree with minimal debt improves your students' life chances. Once students and parents appreciate and then target outcome #3, more motivated behavior follows. Your subsequent wins will derive in part from this well-conceived, well-executed Mission.

WHY WOULD THE MISSION STATEMENT MOTIVATE STUDENTS, PARENTS, AND THE COMMUNITY OUTSIDE OF SCHOOL?

Success is 90 percent discipline. Talent and luck do matter to some degree, but success is primarily the product of discipline.

Successful musicians have discipline; those who quit in grade school have less. Successful broadcasters may have had some good fortune and talent to get their chance, but arriving at and staying at the top requires sustained discipline. Jim Rome, Conan O'Brien, Rush Limbaugh, Colin Cowherd, and Jon Stewart work very hard.

If there is such a strong correlation between discipline and success, why isn't everyone disciplined? It's pretty simple. Discipline requires extra effort today for a payoff "tomorrow." To exert extra effort today, people need a picture, a clear understanding of the future payoff. Some "perfectionists" choose extra effort over less effort for its own sake. But discipline usually requires seeing the future benefit and choosing it and the effort required to get there.

Playing piano takes more work than texting or playing Candy Crush. Those who choose to play piano see a future playing self-created music as worth the effort.

Thankfully there are fun and rewards along the way, but primarily the lure of meaningful future success pushes the diver to train early in the morning, the businesswoman to work late, the applicant to do research for and practice the interview.

Discipline requires extra effort today for a payoff "tomorrow." To exert extra effort today, people need a picture, a clear understanding of the future payoff.

Students are no exception. Students will be more disciplined in school if they have a clear picture and understanding of a resulting more successful future. The Mission gives them that picture, showing them the less difficult, more successful adulthood that should follow a two- or four-year college degree with minimal debt. That picture, that vivid goal, gets them interested in the specific steps to get there. For students raised in families that value school and college, discipline in school may be a family habit. For countless other students, the *Reaching Higher* Mission—the why we should and how we can become two- or four-year college graduates with minimal debt—reinforces and creates the discipline needed to get there.

Without the Mission, students will likely have to love the topic and/or the teacher to try hard.

III

WHY CREATE COLLEGE GRADUATES WITH MINIMAL DEBT?

This is absolutely the wrong time in human history to question education's value. Slackers sleep-walking through their middle and high school years will soon confront a hyper-competitive, global, capitalistic economy.

Every educator should be able to explain succinctly why college graduation with minimal debt improves a student's life chances—higher lifetime earnings, better health, longer life expectancy, among many other preferred outcomes. When I share the story in huge high school auditoriums, you can hear the ventilation humming. Even the most cynical fall silent in momentary contemplation of choices past and present.

HERE'S THE STORY.
CREATE YOUR OWN SYNTHESIZED VERSION.

Your students' parents and you had one source of competition for gainful employment: fellow domestic workers. Students today will soon confront three potent competitors: fellow domestic workers, low wage foreign workers, and intelligent machines. These last two enjoy significant cost advantages. Plus, with time, foreign workers and intelligent machines become more capable, more plentiful, and less expensive.

Let's start with foreign workers. Countless manufacturing jobs have gone abroad. The town of DeWitt, Nebraska, once housed the company that makes that invaluable tool, the Vice-Grip. In the late 1980s, 850 workers streamed daily into this town of 600 to make the world's best pliers. Today, Vice-Grips are made in a city across the river from Hong Kong. The Chinese average manufacturing wage in 2009 was $1.74 per hour.[17] Chinese workers often live in dormitories within industrial compounds and work 12-hour shifts. Today vast manufacturing plants sit in DeWitt, seeking tenants.

Apple® and Walmart once boasted that their products were made in America. Today, few are.

"Why can't that work come home?" President Obama asked Apple CEO Steve Jobs at a February, 2011 dinner. Jobs replied: "Those jobs aren't coming back."[18]

US employers today have billions of inexpensive foreign workers available to hire. Any student beyond 3rd grade unaware of this fierce foreign competitive force suffers from naïveté. Any student or parent unmindful of how the world has changed since mom and dad left high school may be much less motivated than he otherwise would be.

In 2014, I spoke to a high school careers class about how our new economic reality demanded robust knowledge and skill, signaling the increased importance of graduating from college with minimal debt. Suddenly a boy loudly interrupted, "Why didn't they tell us this? I never knew any of this." At the end of class he went to his teacher and asked what he needed to do to raise his failing grade.

Competition breeds effort.
Effort precedes results. Ignorance is not bliss.

Foreign workers are increasingly skilled. By 2020, China is expected to produce 29 percent of all higher education graduates aged 25-34, India 12 percent, and the United States 11 percent— down from 14 percent in 2010.[19]

Inexpensive, plentiful, and skilled foreign workers available for hire have transformed education's relevance. A two- or four-year college degree with minimal debt is a proven path to valuable skills and knowledge, vital attributes to compete against less expensive foreign labor.

But foreign workers available for hire are only part of the story. Let's turn to technology's impact. Advanced engineering, lighter and more powerful materials, and experience enable intelligent machines to be more intelligent, less expensive, and more capable. We can check ourselves out of a Walmart using a machine. We can check ourselves onto an airplane using a machine. Those used to be employees who were raising families and paying rents or mortgages.

Henry Ford made cars with humans. Tesla Motors makes cars with robots.

The agriculture industry in the late 1800s employed roughly 70 percent of US workers.[20] Today it employs 1.5 percent of US workers.[21] And no, we're not eating less—bad guess. USDA data show that average daily calorie intake increased by 24.5 percent, or about 530 calories per day, between 1970 and 2000 alone.[22] Tractors and combines are simply more efficient than humans at tilling crops.

Entire professions have been automated. The paralegal profession is at risk of going the way of the travel agency business: largely replaced by technology that is less expensive and more efficient at performing the task. The Cable TV industry looks poised to follow Blockbuster Video stores and countless music companies into the internet-created cemetery filled with former iconic brands and industries.

Henry Ford made cars with humans.
Tesla Motors makes cars with robots.

While former *New York Times* columnist Bob Herbert describes the trend as "the wholesale replacement of live workers by machines,"[23] what we have seen to date pales in comparison to the future. Robots and increasingly intelligent machines will accelerate that trend.

Intelligent machines and robotics have grown exponentially from a $5.6 billion market in 1995 to projections of $66.4 billion by 2025.[24] And these machines are already performing jobs once done exclusively by human workers: pharmacists, lawyers, drivers, astronauts, store clerks, soldiers, babysitters, and sportswriters.[25]

Former US Treasury Secretary Lawrence Summers writes, "A generation from now, taxis will not have drivers; checkout from any kind of retail establishment will be automatic; call centers will have been automated with voice-recognition technology; routine news stories will be written by bots; counseling will be delivered by expert systems; financial analysis will be done by software; single teachers will reach hundreds of thousands of students, and software will provide them with homework assignments customized to their strengths and weaknesses."[26] A 2013 Oxford Study predicts that 47 percent of today's jobs could be automated within twenty years.[27]

Robin Hanson, an associate professor of economics at George Mason University writes, "Improving machines have two effects on human labor. First, machines get better at the tasks machines do best, which makes doing all the other tasks well, more valuable. This complementary effect raises the demand for skilled human labor. Second, some marginal tasks switch from humans to machines. This substitution effect lowers the demand for human labor."[28]

What Hanson suggests is that advancing technology and intelligent machines create two groups: people capable of creating, maintaining, and utilizing these machines and those vulnerable to replacement by them.

If only apathetic high school students could sit next to an ex-autoworker in a community college class. That thirty-year-old, who lost his job to a machine, has mouths to feed and a mortgage payment. He's not checking his cell phone like Pavlov's dog. He's not distracting others. He's completing the college education he never thought he needed. But that was before the world changed.

And one reason so few students realize that the world has changed is that their immediate environment, school, is largely unaffected by technology and foreign labor. We deliver education today largely as

we did in the past. And I'm not suggesting we change—technology investments have often resulted in no measurable improvements in academic outcomes, creating distractions along with opportunities.[29] Regardless, we need to explain clearly to students how the world beyond school has greatly changed, making school more critical.

Those with skills and knowledge can leverage intelligent machines and inexpensive foreign labor. Those students too disengaged to accumulate valuable skills and knowledge can enter the work force, but they will be forever threatened by the potent confluence of intelligent machines and inexpensive foreign labor.

So Billy can get a job in fast food, a coffee shop, the local cookie company, or the oil lube shop. And these are all dignified jobs, but they pay comparably little for a reason. About 60 percent of US adults age twenty-five and older do not have a two- or four-year college degree.[30] So the majority of US adults go after these easier-to-learn jobs, putting downward pressure on salaries. Meanwhile, robots are also entering these professions. Billy's starting salary may never see a meaningful increase.

Students who can get a $12 an hour job right out of high school and believe this to be their best option should think about whether that job will even be around in 15 years, when they hit the ripe old age of thirty three.

A two-year degree in auto mechanics bears more fruit than an out-of-high-school oil-changing job. A two-year degree should cost about $10,000 in tuition total, while adding thousands to the average salary annually.

A disinterested student recently told me that he didn't need to take the ACT because he's nearly done with his semi-truck driving certificate. I congratulated him on his valuable skill, but reminded him that Google already has developed robot driven cars. "Do I think we'll have robot-driven 18-wheelers by 2020? Probably not.

By 2025? Maybe. By 2030? Absolutely. Robots can drive every hour without rest stops. Robots don't unionize. Robots don't ask for pay raises, retirement benefits, or vacation. Robots don't file workers' comp claims. If you can just get a two-year vocational degree and drive an 18-wheeler, you'll be able to adjust more easily if technology targets truck driving as the next profession to automate."

He sat up, suddenly becoming a less promising prospective customer for local chiropractors. I wondered if he would have paid more attention throughout high school if he had just understood sooner.

The pace of automation is accelerating. In fact, "Less than ten years ago, in the chapter *Why People Still Matter*, (Frank) Levy and (Richard) Murnane (2004)[31] pointed at the difficulties of replicating human perception, asserting that driving in traffic is insusceptible to automation. Six years later, in October 2010, Google announced that it had modified several Toyota Priuses to be fully autonomous."[32]

One of today's iPhones is more powerful than the world's most powerful computer in 1985.[33] The iPhone invented the apps industry in 2007. Apps will be nearly a $38 billion annual industry by 2015.[34] Twitter was invented in 2005. Long-time dictators in Tunisia, Egypt, and Libya had no idea then that it would help overthrow their regimes. The world that many students see as static is hyper-dynamic.

The world that many students see as static is hyper-dynamic. Intelligent machines and low-cost foreign workers have hollowed out America's big middle class hammock that used to catch many of our academically less interested..

Intelligent machines and inexpensive foreign workers have hollowed out America's big middle class hammock that used to catch many of our academically less interested. Today that hammock is frayed and shrunken. Nearly 60 percent of the jobs lost during the recession (of 2008-09) were middle-wage.[35] However, since the recession, only 22 percent of those jobs have been recovered,[36] pushing those without skills and knowledge to working class (living check to check) or worse, public assistance. Since the year 2000, the United States has lost a staggering 32 percent of its manufacturing jobs, the bedrock profession of the middle class. Today, only 9 percent of the jobs in the United States are manufacturing jobs. [37]

In 1981, 59 percent of American adults were classified as middle income, which means between two-thirds and double the nation's median income. In 2011, only 51 percent were middle income. And, "in those thirty years, the 'middle' group's share of the national income pie fell from 60 percent to 45

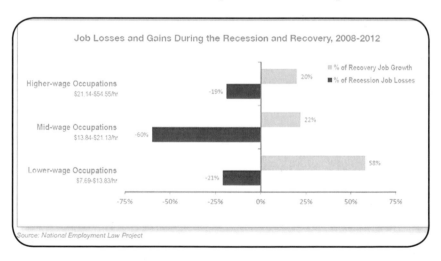

In the 2008 -2012 recession and recovery, the majority of the jobs lost were Mid-wage and the majority of the jobs added were Lower-wage. Skills and knowledge matter more now to avoid lower-wage jobs.

percent."[38] According to a 2010 survey, 55 percent of Americans are living paycheck to paycheck.[39]

In fact, "About three-quarters of the jobs created in the US since the great recession pay $13.52 an hour or less. There is no longer a steady, secure life somewhere in the middle—average is over."[40] The current and future economy is a "hyper-meritocracy."[41]

But sharing this message of a changing world should not motivate solely through fear. Automation and foreign labor aren't necessarily bad. They offer new opportunities. Change creates winners and losers. The winners have valuable knowledge and skills to leverage technology and globalization. A person's perspective reflects his effort and training. School and college matter more than ever.

The confident and prepared embrace today's hypercompetitive world filled with opportunity, especially those enjoying first-world economic advantages. In Henry Ford's time, building a company required immense capital and connections, huge barriers to entry. Evan Williams co-founded Twitter with some basic computers in a San Francisco office. After growing up on a farm near Clarks, Nebraska, he grew his net worth to $2 billion in his early forties.

At one time, ascending the economic ladder took years and patience. Kevin Systrom, a 28-year-old, earned $400 million in 18 months thanks to a tech idea. The Instagram founder sold the company to Facebook for $1 billion in 2012.[42] The unflinching march of technology and foreign labor offer opportunity—and motivation.

Few of my friends saw my hometown of Lincoln, Nebraska, as a good place to start our post-college careers because rising to positions of leadership took so long then in a city full of insurance, real estate, law, manufacturing, medical, and government jobs. Today, Lincoln has burgeoning young companies—Hudl, ArchRival, Licor, Firestream, and others—led by young people.

Technology and low-cost foreign labor provide inexpensive means of production, huge opportunities for entrepreneurs.

More so than ever, "success comes to the prepared mind. Success is not like rain that falls from the sky equally upon everyone."[42]

PROVEN PATHWAYS TO VALUABLE SKILLS AND KNOWLEDGE

A two-year community college degree can offer the necessary preparation. A community college graduate with a welding degree knows that new welding software and high-tech gadgets will only make her more productive.

In fact, a two-year welding degree leads to at least a $35,000 a year job. At age twenty, she'll be looking for a house, rather than an apartment, letting her roommates help pay for the mortgage, not the rent.

The two lead chefs at an excellent local restaurant, Henry's, are young graduates of our local two-year Southeast Community College Culinary Arts program. A two-year degree can be a short, affordable path to a well-paying, fulfilling career with sturdy job security.

A four-year college graduate with minimal to zero debt should also be similarly opportunistic. Intelligent machines and low-cost foreign labor shouldn't threaten a psychology major. With her contacts, knowledge, and so many inexpensive means of production at her disposal, maybe she doesn't even apply for a job—she starts a company. As an owner, she can benefit from low-cost global and automated production. As an employee she is likely to compete against it.

On February 6, 2014, the *Wall Street Journal* reported, "More than one in six men aged twenty-five to fifty-four don't have jobs—a total of 10.4 million. Some had jobs that went overseas or were lost to technology. Having so many men out of work is a chronic condition that shows how technology and globalization are transforming jobs faster than many workers can adapt. Of the 10.4 million unemployed men, 75 percent stopped going to school somewhere short of a 2-year degree."[43]

We haven't seen these unemployment rates for adult males since the 1930s. Right out of high school, many of my contemporaries took solid middle class manufacturing and agriculture jobs—and then the world changed.

Harvard Professor Paul Reville, the former Massachusetts Secretary of Education, put it this way: "Our economy is only going to grow if we grow the kinds of high skills/high knowledge jobs for which others are willing to pay Americans at the standard of living for which we have become accustomed. The only way we're going to be able to do that is if we have our children coming out of school with the knowledge and skills able to drive these high knowledge/high skills businesses."[44]

There's a reason it's called a "knowledge economy."

School is our economic launching pad. Armed with an understanding of the stakes, young people become motivated,

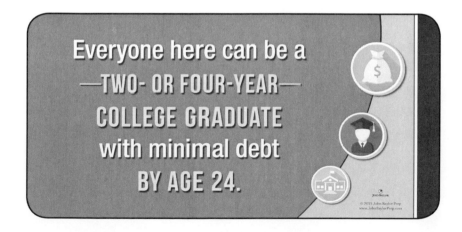

realizing that they can leverage the knowledge and skills readily taught in high school and college into promising careers. School is a legal casino—with the odds in the student's favor.

DJ Weddle, a high school principal, says that the Mission confirming the importance of college "has had a huge impact on our kids wanting to take more advanced classes. Our students are much more engaged in their academics than they were before."[45]

Greg Sjuts, a district superintendent, says that after planting the college message, "The discussions are about increasing their GPAs and ACT scores to earn scholarships instead of paying full price for a college education."

And the Mission should resonate with parents as well once they understand how economic realities have changed. When they left school for work, they had one primary competitor for gainful employment: fellow domestic workers. Today's students will confront three: fellow domestic workers, inexpensive foreign ones, and intelligent machines. Parents, armed with the reason for the Mission, should push their students much more to succeed in school. A permissive, indifferent parent may be unreceptive to the entreaties of an exasperated teacher. But a parent in a school district that champions college graduation should understand why school is an economic trampoline and work to eliminate their children's indifference, tardiness, truancy, misbehavior, and homework defiance.

So rather than hope our school cultures project this critical message to all students, Kindergarten through twelfth grade, let's actually rebrand our schools. "We create two- and four-year college graduates with minimal debt." That coordinated message, regularly expressed verbally and visibly at schools, at every grade, leads to more motivated students. I've seen it.

Now back to those three possible outcomes for your students. How do the other two outcomes work out?

As just discussed, Outcome #3, College Graduate with Minimal Debt, motivates your current students and turns them into opportunists, capable of leveraging intelligent machines and foreign labor, unburdened by large monthly debt payments.

Outcome #2, College Graduate with Much Debt, turns these students into young adults with $300-plus monthly student loan payments into their thirties. They'll be less likely to build the wealth that undergirds the confidence and ignites the freedom to take healthy risks, like starting a company and creating jobs rather than clinging to one due to risk-numbing personal debt. These college graduates should have skills and knowledge, but may be too financially inhibited to maximize opportunities.

They also might be enduring the shame of living at home with mom and dad. A full 36 percent of US adults ages 23 to 31 are back at home with their parents.[46] You might market the *Reaching Higher* Mission as "Operation Keep the Kids from Moving Back into the Basement."

The average amount of debt for a four-year college graduate—at graduation—is $30,000.[47] A young person starts making his loan payments six months after he stops being a full-time student. $30,000 of debt means about $300 in monthly loan payments through about age 32. That's a nine-year ball and chain.

Benjamin, an eighteen-year-old from South Berwick, Maine, applied Early Decision to Tufts University. He began in the Fall of 2014, receiving about $30,000 in scholarships in his freshman year, about half of Tuft's $61,000-a-year retail sticker price. His parents say that they had saved about $30,000 total. So Benjamin and his parents have year one covered.

But even if the numbers stay the same (often costs go up while aid goes down after freshman year), Benjamin will have about $90,000 in debt upon graduation, which means he'll pay about $400 a month through age forty-two. Yikes. The summer before he even left for his dream college, Benjamin admitted, "It's really ridiculous that college costs so much money."[48]

It doesn't have to. Benjamin realized belatedly that it's not merely about becoming a college graduate—it's about doing so with minimal debt. He should have had comparable, less expensive options. And Tufts should be ashamed if it doesn't significantly increase Benjamin's annual scholarship—ashamed for forcing a young man to shoulder so much debt as he heads into adulthood.

Molly graduated from her Illinois high school in 2009 with "average grades" and a 23 on her ACT (the national average is 21.0, and the Illinois average is 20.6). She only looked at Western Illinois and Illinois State University. She chose ISU at the full price of $21,000 to $22,000 a year for Illinois residents.

Molly's family had no college savings for her. Molly borrowed the full amount, graduating in 4.5 years with a Recreation Management degree.

She now has about $100,000 in debt. She personally pays about $750 a month; her parents pay another $400 to $500 a month. They hope the debt is paid off within nine years. Molly lives with her parents back at her childhood home. She is an optimistic, poised, hard-working young woman with a temporary job for her town's park district as she seeks her dream job with the Department of Natural Resources.

"I feel angry. I could buy a house for $100,000. And here I am living with my parents. Not that I would give up my college experience, but I'm not sure it was worth $100,000 in debt. My freshman and sophomore year, I didn't give my debt any thought. I just figured that this is what everyone is doing—this is what you're supposed to do. By junior year I started to get more frustrated because I realized that not everyone does this—other people have saved up money or have been awarded scholarships."

Molly's counselor urged her to look at less expensive four-year colleges. Bemidji State, Northwest Missouri State, Central Michigan, Weber State, and many others would have been less than $14,000 per year back then for her. Molly could have earned $5,000 and borrowed $5,000 a year, leaving a manageable amount annually for her parents. If so, she would have less than $20,000 in debt right now.

Molly attended an excellent, large public high school and had a fine high school experience, playing sports and acting in school plays. But she admits that she did not focus on her schoolwork seriously.

"If I could go back to high school, I'd try to save more money myself. I'd try to find another way to get scholarships or aid so it wouldn't have cost me so much in the long run." A coordinated school Mission championing college graduation with minimal debt may have made Molly a more motivated high school student and a less indebted adult.

Counselors and all staff can inform students and parents about the pitfalls of incurring more than $20,000 in student debt. The *Wall Street Journal* reported that 70 percent of the college class of 2014 would graduate with an average debt of $33,000 per borrower.[49] The average repayment period on student loans has increased from 7.4 years in 1992 to 13.4 years in 2014. In August 2014, less than half of student borrowers were paying their federal loans back on time, with defaults on the rise.[50]

Counselors can publicize the colleges that provide solid four-year educations for less than $22,000 a year—Central Michigan, North Dakota State, Chadron State (Nebraska), South Dakota, Missouri Southern, Wayne State (Nebraska), Bemidji State (Minnesota), Weber State (Utah), and Southern Mississippi are just some of dozens of examples for residents of any state. The list grows for students with higher GPAs and higher ACT or SAT scores.

Many public universities offer below $22,000 yearly price tags for their own state residents. (Still, as we arm our students with the resolve and ability to get the degree on time, we should also mention that fully 68 percent of students at public institutions do not graduate in four years, and 44 percent fail to graduate in six.[51])

As educators, we must expose the myth that college will necessarily saddle young adults with burdensome debt. We can turn our students into motivated, smart, savvy college shoppers. Young people and their parents typically respond to big financial incentives.

Monthly student debt payments have joined monthly health insurance payments as another life-inhibiting expense. While the need for affordable healthcare keeps millions of Americans chained to jobs they dislike, so too do oppressive monthly student loan payments.

A recent survey from American Student Assistance found that "those with student debt are delaying decisions to buy a home, get married, have children, save for retirement, and enter a desired career field because of their debt. This downward spiral has a cascading impact on the nation's economy as the Millennials charged with investing in the nation's future delay their lives because of student debt."[52]

Zack, a thirty-year-old Florida lawyer with $175,000 in student loans from college and law school, laments, "Everyone says that it's a great time to buy a house. But that is not an option right now, thanks to $800 a month in student loan payments. I find myself living paycheck to paycheck."

He is also engaged, but has postponed marriage. "There's no way I can pay for a dream wedding, or even just a regular wedding. I feel like I'm putting my entire life on hold."[53]

Dave Ramsey, the popular money advisor and radio host with whom I often agree, advocates no borrowing for college. I say no more than $5,000 a year for four years: $20,000 in debt means about $215 a month in payments through age thirty one. Sure, your students may not be able to afford the smartest phone, but dumber phones work— and have fewer distractions. Maybe in their twenties they can get by on free TV channels or share an apartment to cut costs. These are modest, non-life-altering sacrifices. Student debt is real, but $215 a month for eight years shouldn't sabotage anyone's plans.

I recently heard a rule of thumb on student borrowing on the NPR radio show *Market Place*: "Borrow no more than your expected first-year salary after college."

What if a student expected to earn $60,000 that first year but settled on a $35,000 a year job? Ouch. And $50,000 in debt means about $400 a month through age thirty four—so much for looking for work in New Zealand, taking that job with a non-profit, or trying to be a professional actor. Enjoy that cubicle throughout your twenties. "Borrow no more than your expected first year salary after college" sounds like advice created by colleges seeking to fund their pricey business models on the backs of naïve students.

Jaws drop in class when Erica Holton, a terrific English teacher at Huntley High School, describes her husband's debt: "Every month, we pay a minimum of $423 and will be lucky to pay off his student loan debt by the time our first son is ready for college. That monthly payment is second only to our mortgage." Now that's love.

What's more, debtors can declare bankruptcy and walk away from mortgages and car loans—but no one can walk away from student loans. Student loan lenders will find debtors in the nursing home if that principal remains unpaid.

I met a 2007 high school graduate now teaching fourth grade. She only took the ACT one time because her score was enough to get into the local state college. But she decided to start in community college to take care of her general requirements less expensively. She ultimately transferred to the local four-year state college and finally graduated in a total of five years, largely because she had changed her major before ultimately settling on elementary education. Despite

having multiple jobs throughout her five years of college, she still has $41,000 in student loan debt at age twenty-six.

"I just wish I had known all this when I was in high school," she told me after she heard the story of how feasible it should be to graduate college with minimal debt. She had received a Kindergarten through twelfth grade education that had no overarching goal that resonated with her, at least none that she had grasped. Untethered to any message from high school, she made mistakes in the ensuing years. She has a good teaching job now, but writes a hefty check each month. Had she had better guidance, she could be building her life today with that money rather than paying off loans.

Adding that prepositional phrase "with minimal debt" to the Mission is critical because among college freshmen with federal student loans, 28 percent don't think they have any federal debt, and 14 percent don't think they have any debt at all. Further, 51 percent of first year student loan borrowers underestimate their debt by more than 10 percent.[54]

If you agree with me that schools and teachers can change the world, this belief bears out only if our students do not become prisoners to their debt.

Outcome #1, No College Degree, typically turns these current students into less-skilled labor, forever vulnerable to increasingly intelligent machines and low-cost foreign labor.

Americans with a four-year college degree made 98 percent more per hour on average in 2013 than those without a degree. That's up from 89 percent five years earlier, 85 percent a decade earlier and 64 percent in the early 1980s.[55]

Four-year college graduates make about $1 million more over a lifetime than high school graduates, while two-year college graduates make about $300,000 more.[56] The reasons may be correlative as well as causal, but economic opportunity lies firmly and increasingly on the side of the college-educated graduate, especially one with minimal to no debt.

People understand money. My fifth grade daughter understands how these two increasingly powerful global forces can be assets or threats. The *Reaching Higher* Mission sells itself. Yet, it still must be packaged succinctly and consistently for maximum persuasive impact.

"We create two- and four-year college graduates with minimal debt"—by visibly and verbally championing the expectation, you get buy in.

And that's exactly what we have to do. Our students' behavior regularly suggests, "So what? Who cares?" And they often won't.

Many won't care about grammar, geometry, geography, or Galileo until they hear how learning about them serves a larger, personally meaningful purpose.

STILL SKEPTICAL THAT GRADUATING FROM COLLEGE WITH MINIMAL DEBT IS A SOCIAL IMPERATIVE, THE ENGINE BEHIND IMPROVING YOUR STUDENTS' FUTURE LIFE CHANCES?

Perhaps these facts will finally persuade those still skeptical. "If a child is born into a family in the lowest economic quintile (meaning a family that earns $28,000 or less), and she doesn't get a college degree, she has only a 14 percent chance of winding up in one of the top two quintiles, and she has a 45 percent chance of never making it out of that bottom bracket. But if she does earn a four-year degree, her prospects change. Suddenly, there is a 40 percent chance that she'll make it into one of the top two quintiles—and just a 16 percent chance that she'll remain stuck at the bottom."[57] The percentages flip based on that degree.

Currently 80 percent of children from top economic quartile families graduate from college, while only 11 percent of children from bottom quartile families graduate from college—a 7.5 to 1 ratio.[58] So step one has to be to regularly inform low-income students that school is their economic launching pad—along with the basics of how to get into a good college at a low cost, an especially realistic prospect for low-income families thanks to need-based aid (if paired with good counseling).

An assistant high school principal at a school with 50 percent poverty rate tells me that nearly 9 percent of her students are truant daily, and at mid-semester nearly one-third of her sophomores are failing two or more classes. A tragic percentage of those students clearly value school less than the alternatives. They have the mind for learning but not the heart.

We learned from the 2015 Baltimore riots that "half of the high school students in the Baltimore Public Schools don't show up for school."[59] Resources weren't the issue: "in 2011 Baltimore ranked second among the nation's largest 100 school districts in how much it spent per pupil, $15,483 per year."[60] There are myriad reasons why too few Baltimore students value education, but if they had regularly heard why education matters so much, coherently and persuasively, it's likely more would have recognized it as the non-negotiable ladder upward.

We teach content often without explaining why it matters. School matters for multiple reasons, especially because it should lead to a proven pathway to true skills, knowledge, and economic opportunity: a two- or four-year college degree with minimal debt. Some, maybe a majority of skeptical students and their parents, would reconsider if they just understood the overarching goal.

However, Kindergarten through twelfth grades cannot just be a 24/7 pep rally for college, because at the same time that college is increasingly critical, it is also increasingly expensive. Together, we can and should arm students and parents with both

1. an appreciation for the increasing relevance of further education and

2. strategies for achieving a college degree most affordably.

THE MARENGO MIRACLE

Marengo, Illinois, rests about 61 miles northwest of downtown Chicago. Marengo's beautiful high school opened in 2004 and serves about 800 students. From 2000 to 2010, the percentage of those students that qualified for Free and Reduced Lunch rose from 3.3 percent to 24.3 percent. By 2013, 36.3 percent of Marengo's High School students qualified for Free and Reduced Lunch.

All Marengo Community High School juniors take the ACT. In April 2009, the school's average ACT had dropped to 19.5. Superintendent Dan Bertrand, Principal Scott Shepard, and the entire staff dug in and intensified the curriculum. An on-staff reading specialist began helping students outside of class; some students attended ACT Prep evening sessions taught by teachers.

In 2009-10, the school began showing to juniors during class the twelve sessions that comprise the John Baylor Prep ACT course. I visited the school in April 2010 to reinforce those lessons and to amplify the importance of attending the best college at the lowest cost.

By 2010-2011, banners announced the school's previous annual average ACT Scores ("Class of 2011, can you beat these?"). College pennants of the schools attended by the prior year's graduates bracketed the counseling office, visible from the main foyer. The three counselors promoted two- and four-year college degrees and scholarships. Students began to push each other to take the ACT four times.

In his October 14, 2011 report to the Board, Dr. Bertrand wrote, "MCHS has ranged from a low of 19.5 to this year's high of 21.5."

Just one year later Marengo's average ACT score had risen to 22.1.

Marengo had developed a plan and executed it well: create a college-going culture that emphasizes graduating with minimal debt. The goal was not merely higher test scores. The goal was college graduates—a goal promoted daily and undergirded by stronger curriculum and important supplements.

Motivation jumped. Teachers and students bought in to the plan. Better academic outcomes, including test scores, followed.

In May 2013, Scott Shepard announced he would be taking the principal's job at a large nearby high school. Dr. Bertrand wrote his staff: "During Scott's tenure we have seen a good school become a great school and excellence has become the standard for all. We have seen MCHS be a "Featured School" at the Raising Student Achievement Conference, test scores rise to a level I am not sure anyone thought was even possible, and MCHS become one of the top 100 (10 percent) of the high schools in the State."

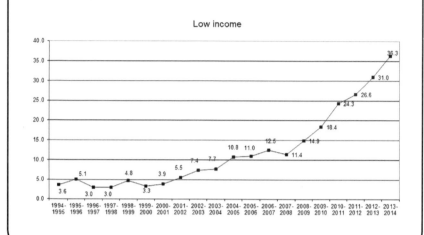

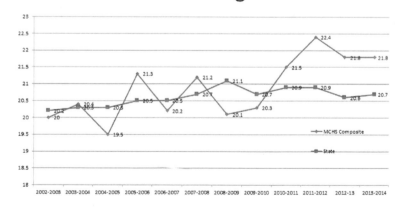

How informing seventh grade students and their parents led to big test score improvements.

We need to educate the parents as much as we educate their students on why college counts. They may become our critical allies at home if they just know what's at stake.

Allen Poynter is the Principal at Hardyville Memorial School, a Kindergarten through eighth grade rural school in Kentucky. Eighty percent of the students are low-income, receiving free and reduced lunch. The national average is 42.9 percent.[61]

Memorial's seventh graders scored very poorly on the Explore Assessment Test in 2010. Allen explains what then happened. "We had to tell parents what these poor scores meant for the future. The parents didn't appreciate the importance of that assessment and its connection with the ACT. I made a personal phone call to each parent. I told them that I am the principal and that we need them to attend a meeting on the importance of the Explore test scores. It wasn't an option. That year we literally had 99 percent of our parents show up. We talked about remediation classes and their pocketbook. And the bottom line was their pocketbook. And we handed each parent their child's score, explaining what it meant. Those were eye-opening moments right there."

"One parent said, 'Why didn't you do this for my older child? I am so glad you told me this.' And she told her son right then and there, 'You are going to do this.'

"We saw improvement, and we attribute that to communicating with parents. You have to call the parents. The kids won't take the information home. They don't want the parents to come, and just as many parents don't want to take the time. I don't want just mommy and daddy here. I want mommy and daddy and Johnny. And there's real accountability. We had them write down a goal with their parents. They wrote a goal for their next year's Explore Test."

Allen says that they still have at least 90-plus percent of the parents showing up each year for this program explaining test scores. "We just tell them—you have to know what these scores mean to you. It's a one-time deal each year."

Those parents understood how those middle school test scores predicted future ACT scores that eventually would affect college choices and costs. Those parents got the Mission and pushed their children to try harder.

"We saw improvement, and we attribute that to communicating with parents. We just tell them—you have to know what these scores mean to you."

What if all faculty and staff echoed the Mission daily?

Allen Poynter also shared this: "I take all my seventh and eighth graders to a college campus; I'm wondering if I need to do it earlier. We communicate not IF you're going to college but WHEN you go to college. Lots of kids have never been outside the state; some have never been to Bowling Green, 40 miles away, and we want to show them that they have options and that there's a big world out there outside of our county."

Memorial school explore test results

Consider the tables below, which have the **same group of students** over the course of two assessments—their seventh grade scores and their eighth grade scores

	2010-2011 (7th Grade)		2011-2012 (8th Grade)
English	50%		74%
Math	13%		36%
Reading	38%		56%
Science	3%		23%
			Parent meeting only
	2011-2012 (7th Grade)		2012-2013 (8th Grade)
English	35%		76%
Math	9%		24%
Reading	26%		40%
Science	0%		18%
			Parent Meeting and John Baylor Prep
	2012-2013 (7th Grade)		2013-2014 (8th Grade)
English	62%		67%
Math	21%		24%
Reading	21%		20%
Science	4%		29%
			Parent Meeting Only

(Vertical center label: Parents learn importance of Explore Results)

Notice that by year three, the seventh graders had gotten the message even before taking their first Explore Test, scoring higher than seventh graders had previously scored in three of the four sections."

IV

LOW-INCOME STUDENTS NEED MORE

Janet has taught for fifteen years in an urban school.

"There's a high level of disrespect towards teachers and staff that is tolerated by the administration. The disrespect can come from the students or their guardians (parents, grandparents, aunts). I feel like some administrators I've worked under have set very low behavior expectations for students just because they come from a low-income household and/or they have problems at home. The tone seems to be it's no big deal to be disrespected or cursed at by a student. I have been called many creative names. 'Bitch ass' was the most common this year."

Few students are born hostile to learning. Somehow their environment hasn't clearly given them a picture of the brighter future learning will create. And the more difficult the home environment, the more important the *Reaching Higher* Mission becomes in school because those students will need even greater discipline for success.

Janet continued, "The principals I've had have tried to improve the situation by bringing in speakers or training the staff in various behavior methods. The only thing I have seen work is having a strong administration that sets high behavior standards for all students and supports their teachers. I worked for one glorious year under one great principal who truly expected all students to be focused on learning and did not tolerate any form of disrespect or disruption in the classroom. She expected her teachers to teach, not be behavior experts. It was the only time I felt like I was really teaching and the students were learning. The test scores validated this.

> *And the more difficult the home environment, the more important the Reaching Higher Mission becomes in school because those students will need even greater discipline for success.*

"Also the students were proud of their school. It was 'cool' to be smart. I love to teach, but that is not what much of my day involves. Much of my day is spent dealing with behavior. If I had had more options financially, there are many times I would have just quit. The administration and the central office need to remember that the students and their families are not the only people who deserve to be treated respectfully; the teachers and the staff deserve to be treated with respect too."

Janet teaches fourth grade. In her school, 82 percent of the students receive free or reduced lunch, well above the national average of 42.9 percent.[62] "With more free and reduced lunch students, you tend to have more behavior issues," she says.

Another teacher in an urban school filled largely with low-income minority students quit the profession after just one year. The students' behavior was hostile and mocking. They swore at her and each other often. The parents were no help. She cried daily. She taught music—in an elementary school. She left teaching to earn a masters degree in music theory from Northwestern.

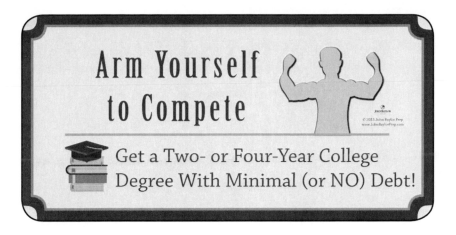

Arm Yourself to Compete

Get a Two- or Four-Year College Degree With Minimal (or NO) Debt!

Children don't emerge from the maternity ward hostile to learning and mocking their friends who try. They are conditioned somehow to deemphasize school. Perhaps their families remain unconvinced of school's potential. Perhaps their parents are overwhelmed. Perhaps the students themselves are unconvinced of their own potential. Perhaps they received too few early learning opportunities before Kindergarten. Perhaps they have no access to after-school enrichment programs. Most likely, it is some combination of multiple factors.

Low income, low scores, and no college degrees in the family are the three "adverse indicators" that minimize the likelihood of college graduation. But K-12 schools armed with the *Reaching Higher* Mission start to attack the self-doubt, apathy, and hostility too commonly associated with these attributes.

Janet says that she and her fellow teachers talk about college as a goal, but there's no coordinated message explaining why and specifically how to get there and how to graduate affordably. Clearly, though, those with low income and no college graduates in the family need more than just the Mission to become college graduates with minimal debt. School policies consistent with that goal are critical. Janet's lone "glorious year" was the one led by the "great principal," who engendered respect for school through discipline and praise. If the Mission is the true goal, policies bolstering the Mission naturally spring—firm discipline addresses behavior antithetical to the Mission while praise accompanies behavior consistent with it.

Paul Tough, in his bestseller, *How Children Succeed*, describes how a low IQ is not the main cause of academic challenge. A chaotic home more often is. Lower income students can come from chaotic and challenging environments away from school. They especially need consistency and high expectations from their teachers. School should be their sanctuary. Accommodating disruptive forces in any school, especially one with many lower-income students, sabotages the order and consistency they seek—and the Mission.

Transforming low-income students— they need more than the Mission

One-third of college students in this country are the first in their families to attend college and only 15 percent of them will graduate within six years.[63] For them and others from low-income families, the Mission from Kindergarten through twelfth grade will help, but it won't turn enough into college graduates with minimal debt.

Many low-income students lack belief in their own ability. Too many are afflicted with what Stanford Professor Carol Dweck calls a *Fixed Mindset*, the belief that ability is finite and that challenges simply reveal the mind's limited potential. Thus, social or academic adversity is probably permanent—revealing limited potential and reinforcing self-doubt. How sad and wrong! Those armed with academic success as a family heirloom typically possess the *Growth Mindset*, correctly seeing the mind as elastic, capable of overcoming temporary setbacks.

Instilling this understanding that the brain is like a muscle, ever-growing thanks to challenge and exercise, can inculcate the persistence and belief that too many young people lack. Replacing the *Fixed Mindset* with the *Growth Mindset* creates grit, leading to more ambitious, confident, and successful students.

Sharing a simple message about the impermanence of adversity can have a big effect, especially on your low-income students. To embolden disadvantaged students, I encourage educators and former students to regularly share stories about how high school and early college years can be challenging and often discouraging,

Replacing the Fixed Mindset with the Growth Mindset creates grit, leading to more ambitious, confident, and successful students.

but with time, confidence and success can return. One high school teacher tells me that each Friday she lets her students ask her one personal question about herself. Her students understand how she overcame obstacles that she once thought were permanent.

Patty G., a long-time college counselor adds this: "I don't believe that families in poverty understand debt. They pay in cash. My students will not borrow money even to pay for college. They will drop out and work until they can afford college. We have to do a better job in helping these students understand the financial aspects of earning a college education and managing money. Also, families in poverty sometimes will sabotage any member of the family who wants to leave the family lifestyle. He cannot be 'better than' the rest of the family. Family is most important. In order for these students to be successful in college, they have to leave their family behind for those years. That is very difficult unless they have a 'new family' that they trust even more than their biological family. Sometimes there is a glimmer of hope and the students choose to break the cycle. Someone or a group of caring adults makes a difference in those lives."

This scenario sometimes stems from different cultures emphasizing different values. For example, Hispanic students can be skeptical of college because of their wonderful instinct to immediately help their family financially. I start by asking them, "Imagine how much more financially helpful you could be with a college degree and minimal debt?"

Bottom line, only 11 percent of children from bottom quartile families currently graduate from college. So amplifying the importance and possibility of graduating with minimal debt is step one. Successfully executing that goal will also require a devoted, coordinated, school-wide effort attacking what has held back too many students: skepticism about college's impact, naïveté about how low their annual net cost can be, fear of borrowing even $5,000 a year, a fixed mindset, cultural biases, and uncertainty about how college with minimal debt can help them help their family.

You might call this additional effort: "The *Reaching Higher* Mission: enhanced version." Much research demonstrates the need for the enhanced version of the Mission, especially for our low-income students.

THE KALAMAZOO PROMISE:

Begun in November 2005, the *Kalamazoo Promise* pays full tuition at a two-year or four-year Michigan Public College for any Kalamazoo Public School (KPS) graduate. Participating colleges include the University of Michigan, Michigan State, Western Michigan, Central Michigan—you get the idea.

Michelle Miller Adams, author of *The Power of a Promise: Education and Economic Renewal in Kalamazoo*, says that the initial anonymous donors wanted to do more than help young people become college graduates. "They wanted to strengthen and invigorate the school district, and they were also seeking to make Kalamazoo a more attractive place to live and work."[64]

The Promise increased the percentage of KPS graduates attending a Michigan public 4-year college from about 30 percent to about 44 percent.[65] Erica Adams, a 2012 Michigan State graduate and KPS graduate, explained that The Promise changed her ambitions and made it possible for her to plan for a Big Ten school rather than a community college.[66] Now a state foster care specialist, she visits middle schools in Kalamazoo and sees examples of a new, strong college-bound culture. At a Kalamazoo middle school she saw a huge banner in the main entrance. "There was a huge check on the wall, a $50,000 check, that said, 'Put your name here'."

Despite such progress since 2005, the *Kalamazoo Promise* has barely changed KPS' high school graduation rate. For low-income populations, the Mission—even accompanied by free college tuition—has not yet been enough.

McHenry County Community College in Illinois created its own Promise: all recent graduates from the county could attend MCC for free. MCC's Promise lasted just one year because it flooded MCC with unprepared, unmotivated students.

'Free' doesn't seem to work. Many students have to have some minimal financial investment to establish accountability. An understanding of the value of college also would help create true extrinsic motivation.

Why wouldn't free tuition for college increase high school and college graduation rates among low-income students? A stubborn problem requires a more involved solution. "Students scoring in the 1100 to 1199 range on their SATs have a 2 in 3 chance of graduating with a four-year degree if they come from the top income quartile. If they come from families in the bottom quartile, they have just a 1 in 5 chance."[67]

University of Texas experiments may have an answer to what can yield more low-income college graduates, beyond the Mission.

- Again, there are three "adversity indicators" harming the likelihood of graduation: low income, low high school test scores, and first generation college student.

- Students with "adversity indicators" often lack both a strong sense of belonging, and they do not believe that struggles are temporary and can be overcome. The University of Texas provides students with two or more of the three "adversity indicators" with stories from faculty or former graduates about how they too struggled academically and felt they didn't belong freshman year—but how college for them improved. Simply reading these stories increased the percentage of disadvantaged freshmen completing at least twelve credits that first semester from 82 percent to 86 percent.

- The UT researchers have conducted similar experiments at other colleges, all with the same results. Students with some or all of the three "adversity indicators" do better when exposed—even briefly—to messages about the brain's ability for growth and the temporary nature of adversity.

- "Sure, they still feel bad when they fail a test or get in a fight with a roommate or are turned down for a date. But in general, they don't interpret those setbacks as a sign that they don't belong in college or that they're not going to succeed there. It is only students facing the particular fears and anxieties and experiences of exclusion that come with being a minority—whether by race or by class—who are susceptible to this problem. Those students often misinterpret temporary setbacks as a permanent indication that they can't succeed or don't belong at UT. For those students, the intervention can work as a kind of inoculation. And when, six months or two years later, the germs of self-doubt try to infect them, the lingering effect of the intervention allows them to shrug off those doubts exactly the way the advantaged students do."[68]

This message of belonging and the fleeting nature of adversity needs to become part of the *Kalamazoo Promise* and similarly well-intentioned efforts. In fact, all high schools can instill this sense of belonging and the sense that the mind can adapt and overcome—replacing the *Fixed Mindset* with the *Growth Mindset*. Teachers and former students sharing stories of their own college journey to confidence and success can make believable for all the goal of college graduation with minimal debt. No lower-income student should head to college still questioning whether he belongs there or has the brain to graduate. Coordinated messaging can instill this *growth mindset*.

STUDY SKILLS AND COMMUNITY SERVICE CAN ALSO HELP THE LESS AFFLUENT.

Tulsa Achieve provides two free years of Community College for all Tulsa County residents. The last class each day is a Strategies for Academic Success class, when the participating community college students get homework help. Students also participate in two years of community service—so that there is a cost, though not monetary. Students need to have some cost. While nationally only 30 percent of community college students graduate within three years,[69] *Tulsa Achieve* has an 80 percent graduation rate.

URBAN PREP:

In Chicago only about half of all students are accepted to any college, and African-American males have a 40 percent high school graduation rate.[70] But the story of *Urban Prep*, a school focused on helping African-American boys, brings hope.

Amanda Paulson in *The Christian Science Monitor* writes, "The most notable aspect of *Urban Prep*'s culture is its focus on college, an emphasis that infuses every aspect of the school—from an achievement-oriented creed that students recite daily, to the framed acceptance letters that decorate the walls. 'Every single adult in the building—from the director of finance that handles payroll, to the CEO, to all the teachers—has a very clear understanding that our Mission is to get students to college,' says Kenneth Hutchinson, the school's director of college counseling. 'We start in the freshman year. It's not about helping them fill out applications; it's about building strong applicants.'"[71] *Urban Prep*'s students have a 100 percent college acceptance rate.

The Mission, Graduate from College with Minimal Debt, motivates all. Those with "adversity indicators" also need a message of belonging and adversity's short-lived nature— a focused effort to transform the *Fixed Mindset* to the *Growth Mindset*.

V

THE DETRACTORS
AND COLLEGE SKEPTICS

Some educators instinctively get the benefits of this Mission: "We create two- and four-year college graduates with minimal debt."

Others seem to have seven primary objections:

1. It's not inclusive.

   a. We all know high school students with grave holes in their academic foundation, making college an unlikely prospect. And there may be upperclassmen incapable of meeting this goal—when announced. However, those saying this Mission is not inclusive are effectively saying it's beyond many students, including current elementary and middle school students. Do we really want to give up on lower income second graders? "Hello parents. We're not embracing college graduation with minimal debt for your children because we think it's beyond many of you." How sad—and unfair.

   b. It's the exact opposite. Believing that any of our elementary school students are unlikely future college graduates excludes them from the goals shared by so many parents. This belief really hurts because people, especially children, typically reflect the immediate environment's expectations. If the teacher herself assumes that many first graders cannot eventually become college graduates, many children and their parents may absorb that expectation. The soft prejudice of low expectations is wrong, but especially regarding a goal that is so achievable and important.

c. Our culture typically fails at turning children born into the lowest economic quartile into college graduates: only one out of nine gets there. It is less likely for bright children from poor families to finish college than less able children from affluent families to finish college. Unacceptable. That moral imperative alone is reason to embrace this goal, including the disadvantaged in a district-wide Mission that closely correlates with their future economic interests.

d. And with more and more colleges catering now to students with Special Needs and Learning Disabilities, all students can do this.

2. <u>It's not feasible</u>.

a. Rather than wondering how exactly to make this goal a reality for all students, some educators doubt that it's possible. Even public universities cost $13,000 to $35,000 per year for in-state residents. But these are the retail sticker prices that dominate the media headlines. The actual net cost, adjusted for inflation, has varied little. Looking only at tuition and fees, the inflation-adjusted net price is actually lower than it was a decade ago.[72] And, of course, lower-income students should qualify for not just merit-based aid, but also need-based aid: the abundance of scholarship money targeting families earning less than $75,000 a year—often even more.

b. Such skepticism demonstrates the importance of teaching all educators the basics regarding how students can get into their best fit college at the lowest cost. A simple understanding of how college admissions and financial aid work should strengthen all educators' belief in the Mission to create college graduates with minimal debt.

3. <u>School shouldn't be about getting a degree. It should be about getting an education.</u>

a. This argument assumes the two goals are mutually exclusive. In fact, getting an education is the preferred means to the end, a college degree with minimal debt. Establishing the end goal should trigger healthy discussions regarding how best to get there—in this case, encouraging students to find and cultivate productive passions within school to inspire the desire to learn and deeply engage: the essence of true education. Currently with little emphasis on college graduation with minimal debt, there is little context that would naturally encourage conversations about getting a true education en route. Plant this garden, and there will be so much to harvest.

4. <u>College is increasingly about partying rather than learning and rigor</u>.

    a. True, many college students receive suspect educations. The rigor is often not what it should be. Colleges have financial incentive to please their students, and inflated grades and easy classes please many. But teaching students simple tactics can mitigate these weaknesses undermining many colleges. Take only small classes. Sit in the front of class. Choose only highly rated professors. Go to the professors' office hours. Avoid those on a five-year beverage fest (See page 122 for our full list of suggestions for maximizing college).

    b. High school educators can easily share these tips with their students, especially during senior spring. All colleges have good and bad teachers. Along with suspect educations, meaningful educations are available at nearly all colleges. As you arm students to graduate with minimal debt, also arm them with simple tactics to get there.

5. <u>There are good options outside of college</u>.

    a. Vetted, proven, sustained training programs offered by local companies can be good options for students who otherwise might merely launch themselves into the first $10 an hour job they can get after high school. And certain local companies with solid training programs are options that can be later added to the Mission as an alternative path to skills and knowledge. A local for-profit vocational training and credentialing program might similarly receive your promotion—if the quality and cost warrant. Further, by publicizing alternatives to college graduation with minimal debt, schools logically would research local company job-training programs and recommend only the ones that offer the best long-term skill building for students. Currently few school leaders vet or rate training programs offered by local companies or for-profit schools because anything after twelfth grade typically is considered beyond the school's current Mission.

6. Significantly more college graduates will water down the quality and value of the degree.

   a. Currently few hold local two- or four-year colleges accountable for their product. Championing the Mission will ensure that at least local K-12 administrators will. Local community leaders and employers united behind the Mission should as well. And if locally there are shorter, less expensive, skills-intensive employee training or credentialing programs comparable to a two- or four-year degree, the Mission will more likely reveal these alternatives than does our current system of vague, often uncommunicated expectations for students.

7. College doesn't guarantee a good job.

   a. Economist and New York Times columnist Paul Krugman in March 2011 wrote: "It's no longer true that having a college degree guarantees that you'll get a good job, and it's becoming less true with each passing decade."[73]

       No it may not "guarantee" a good job, but it helps a lot. A report, from Georgetown's Center on Education and the Workforce, titled *Recovery-Job Growth and Education Requirements Through 2020* found that "By 2020, 65 percent of all jobs in the economy will require postsecondary education and training beyond high school. Thirty-five percent of the job openings will require at least a bachelor's degree and thirty percent of the job openings will require some college or an associate's degree."[74] Further, employers today often only interview and hire college graduates even if the job doesn't require college training: a process called degree inflation.

Finally, the benefits of college run much deeper than simple economic ROI. We use the economic ROI argument primarily because it's more understandable and quantifiable. Plant that seed and conversations about the true depth of college's benefits ensue.

Before I spoke to her school's eighty seniors on this topic, a counselor told me that three of them were headed straight into the military (rather than first into ROTC, which pays for four years of tuition and a monthly stipend all through college). "But that is a great option for these three," she explained.

I asked to talk to them afterwards.

I thanked them for their courage and patriotism. I also urged them to seek rigorous roles and training while serving, so as to be armed with needed skills and knowledge later in civilian life. I encouraged them to take care of some college credits while enlisted. They each agreed.

College with minimal debt by age 24 is a proven pathway to skills and knowledge, but even those choosing a different path plan better thanks to an understanding of the stakes: the job competition that awaits them.

RETORT TO THE COLLEGE SKEPTICS

The contrarian school of thought has become increasingly visible. Its message goes something like this: college is too expensive and no longer worth the time and cost. UnCollege and other websites such as The Do School[75] and Enstitute[76] advocate hacking one's own education. One way to get a column printed by the *Wall Street Journal* is to question the Return on Investment (ROI) of college itself.

"Will you marry me (and my student loan debt)?"[77]

"High school senior suing parents for college tuition."[78]

"Higher ed becoming a joke."[79]

However, if you read beyond the screaming headline and provocative first paragraph, the column usually laments the high cost of college and its sometimes low expectations—justifiable complaints. I would question the ROI of college as well if I knew a graduate from Northern Ohio University or Wheelock College with $65,000 in debt—that's about $500 a month in student loan payments through age 34. Here's a list of colleges that are good at creating indebted students. Like most colleges, they can offer excellent teachers and educations, but there are less expensive options of similar or better quality.

Us NEWS' LIST OF COLLEGES WITH THE HIGHEST AVERAGE DEBT FOR NEW GRADUATES.[80]

School name (state)	Average debt load, class of 2012	Percentage of students who borrowed	US News rank and category
Wheelock College (MA)	$49,439	82	69, Regional Universities (North)
Anna Maria College (MA)	$49,206	86	Regional Universities (North)
Becker College (MA)	$44,596	94.8	Regional Colleges (North)
Clark Atlanta University	$43,727	93	National Universities
Oral Roberts University (OK)	$43,457	58	54, Regional Universities (West)
Trinity University (TX)	$42,987	46	1, Regional Universities (West)
Quinnipiac University (CT)	$42,730	67	11, Regional Universities (North)
St. Anselm College (NH)	$42,631	79	120, National Liberal Arts Colleges
Mount Ida College (MA)	$42,362	79.7	37, Regional Colleges (North)
Utica College (NY)	$42,303	83	116, Regional Universities (North)

The film *Ivory Tower* spends some time interviewing college detractors, those questioning the return on the financial investment and time. Dale Stephens, the Founder of UnCollege, says, "People say to me all the time, 'Well Dale, aren't you ruining people's lives by encouraging them to take a risk and not go to college?' I think it's much riskier to go to college and take on $20,000 in debt per year and then have miserable job prospects when you get out and have to start repaying that debt. That sounds like a really high risk to me."[81]

Elizabeth Stark, a Mentor for the Thiel Fellowship, which gives $100,000 to twenty brilliant young adults to spend two years pursuing their entrepreneurial or intellectual passion rather than college, says: "There's no longer a great value proposition in paying $200,000 for a college degree, particularly when you're not at an Ivy League School."[82]

I agree with both. However, there are many colleges— Southern Mississippi, University of Maine-Fort Kent, Northwest Missouri State, Truman State (Missouri), University of North Dakota, Montana Western, Wayne State (Nebraska), Ole Miss, University of Alabama-Huntsville, South Dakota State, and dozens of others—that offer solid four-year educations to average high school students for a net cost of under $18,000 a year, often less than $13,000 a year. New College of Florida offers an outstanding, rigorous liberal arts education for under $24,000 a year. Students can comfortably borrow up to $5,000 and earn at least $5,000 each year, leaving the manageable difference for parents or scholarships. These college skeptics malign high-cost colleges apparently unaware that many solid college educations don't require lots of expense or debt.

College contrarians cannot truly feel that most of America's 19-year-olds should live at home and just find their way, "hacking" the skills and knowledge offered by college. I can hear China cheering that genius advice. Do we really want to send the message to America's families that Billy should go right into the workforce at age 19? Probably not.

Peter Thiel himself says, "The Thiel Fellowship is focused on a small subset of people who I think will do fantastic even without a college credential. I think it is a much more difficult question—what one does for people from average backgrounds, less advantaged backgrounds. I don't have answers for it."[83]

Securing marketable knowledge and skills without college may seem less expensive initially. The real expense arises over time in the missed earnings potential.[84]

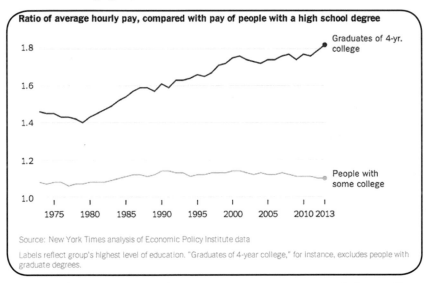

Ratio of average hourly pay, compared with pay of people with a high school degree

Graduates of 4-yr. college

People with some college

Source: New York Times analysis of Economic Policy Institute data

Labels reflect group's highest level of education. "Graduates of 4-year college," for instance, excludes people with graduate degrees.

David Autor, an M.I.T. economist, wrote in 2014 that college costs negative $500,000. College is cheaper than free: even after considering college's cost, not graduating from one will cost you about $500,000.[85]

In the film *Ivory Tower*, Michael Roth, President of Wesleyan University in Connecticut, declares: "Many intellectuals are saying that it would be better if some people don't go to college at all. I think that's an assault on democracy, and it's an attempt to keep people in their place and reinforce social inequality. Education should foster social mobility and the possibility of equality. You've got to be crazy to intentionally not get a college degree if you have a choice today."[86]

Between community colleges, need-based aid, and low-cost, solid four-year colleges, all students have that choice. Adults, especially educators, should persuade them to make it.

Still, there are companies offering worthy training programs to high school seniors—plus other paths to economic security without college. Your unenthused students mention these, so let's examine each.

COMPUTER PROGRAMMING

If Eduardo is truly a computer whiz, capable of writing code on his computer, college may not be critical. Please don't confuse computer gamers with computer programmers—one group is possibly addicted to largely unproductive, anti-social behavior, while Silicon Valley seeks to hire the other. Recent statistics from Iowa State University's Psychology department show that roughly 10 percent of American youth is addicted to video games to an extent that causes social, family, and psychological damage.[87] If Eduardo's primary goal is a high score on *Call of Duty*, he may not be a promising candidate for a college degree or compelling employment options.

In fact, 'coding bootcamps' are increasingly affordable and effective. Real coding skills can be mastered in months at these 'coding bootcamps.' Computer coders would benefit from college training, but they may not need a college degree for promising employment.

Further, the window of opportunity for profitably launching a high tech company can be small. If Mark Zuckerberg had borrowed the Facebook idea from his fellow students months later, it may have been launched elsewhere by someone else. For Zuckerberg, immediately running Facebook full time made more financial sense than finishing his Harvard degree.

However, Bill Gates, Steve Jobs, and Mark Zuckerberg are outliers. There are others, but their numbers are probably in the hundreds, perhaps thousands annually. There are roughly 3,000,000 high school seniors each year in the U.S.[88]

Bill Gates, himself, wrote on his blog in 2015, "Although I dropped out of college and got lucky pursuing a career in software, getting a degree is a much surer path to success. College graduates are more likely to find a rewarding job, earn higher income, and even, evidence shows, live healthier lives than if they didn't have degrees. They also bring training and skills into America's work force, helping our economy grow and stay competitive."

He adds, "It's just too bad that we're not producing more of them."[89]

SALES

If your student eventually sells a good product, few care if she has a college degree. The more technical the product, the more likely someone will ask about her background to gauge credibility. But if she loves to sell, she'll get her shot if she can persuade a business owner that she wants to wake up early each morning, call prospects, set up meetings, experience rejection, inhabit vendor booths at trade shows, and have a sales quota each month and year. Good car sales pros make six figures and often don't have college degrees. Many sales jobs pay less because the product's price is lower; some sales jobs pay more. Just make sure that a young person loves to sell—and doesn't plan on changing her mind.

Here's a valuable story for an aspiring salesman adamantly against post-high school education. Gene Chevalier owns seven Verizon Wireless retail stores. He hired a 23-year-old in 2010. Gene's employee was excellent at sales and worked hard. After two years, Gene decided to mentor this young man. Eventually Gene offered this employee ownership in the business and a compensation package exceeding $100,000 a year.

What's the lesson? If your student truly wants to sell rather than go to college, encourage him to get hired within a small, private business. Every successful entrepreneur goes through a growing phase when he seeks help managing growth. After 17 years of working for First Data, a Fortune 100 company, and now seven running his own business, Gene says, "A strong work ethic alone will put a worker in the top 10 percent. Find an entrepreneur, show him your worth,

Always look for possible destination jobs. In fact, in life, deemphasize choices that are stepping-stones; prioritize those that at least have a chance of sustaining you long term.

and he'll take care of you." Someone so strategically motivated may not need a degree to get the initial opportunity or the long-term career. Further, if he needs more education, he can get it part time while continuing in the business.

Your students can always decide later that a job or relationship was merely a stepping-stone, but it's unlikely a sandwich shop job will be anything else—unless they decide to open some of their own Subway franchises.

The entrepreneur

If a young person has the entrepreneurial gene, she may not need a college degree. But, according to Bloomberg, eight out of ten entrepreneurs who start businesses fail within the first 18 months.[90] So new business prospects can be bleak even with a college degree and the connections, maturity, and financial and accounting knowledge it should bring.

If a student is so inclined and adamantly against college, encourage her to start her first business in high school or soon thereafter. She'll learn a lot. And if it doesn't work out, she'll still have plenty of time to reinvent herself, climb out of any financial losses, and get that college degree for her next conquest.

Eight out of ten entrepreneurs who start businesses fail within the first 18 months.

On the job training programs for workers

There are companies that invest in rigorous training programs so that those with merely high school diplomas can become very capable workers, perhaps workers without any need for additional formal education. An example would be railroad companies, which can pay high school graduates in their early twenties $50,000 to $130,000 a year. But there can be a lot of travel and physical labor, two unwelcome requirements when families and then middle age arrive. Railroad employees with college degrees may have more control over their schedule and travel, plus a greater likelihood of promotion. But high school graduates able to get hired by railroad companies can enjoy upper middle class incomes.

Another pathway to comfortable salaries travels through franchises—from franchise worker to franchise owner. At McDonald's, some 60 percent of owner/operators and regional managers started as hourly employees.[91] Working hard and showing interest may get your high school student promoted from hourly worker to manager with opportunities for ownership. However, fast food restaurants are already automating many tasks previously done by humans until now.[92]

LAW ENFORCEMENT, PUBLIC SAFETY, AND CONSTRUCTION

Some aspiring firemen, police officers, and construction workers believe that college is superfluous. Lincoln (Nebraska) Police Department Captain Genelle Moore says, "We get about 600 applicants per opening. We hire twice a year and hire very few with just the minimum requirements, a high school diploma or GED. I can recall one in the last 15 years. This is pretty standard for the industry. College gives them better critical thinking skills and vocabulary. It doesn't really matter what the two-year or four-year degree is in. Pick something you can be employed in after you retire from here. We have criminal justice majors but more and more with different degrees. We want well-rounded folks because we teach them what we want them to know."

Moore continues, "The Lincoln Fire Department may hire more with merely a high school diploma, though I know they're trying to work towards a more educated force. In the 90s, Lincoln Fire hired once a year and got upwards of 850 to 900 applications

per opening. Since then, they've been getting about 325 to 375 per year for a small number of openings. The paramedics do need some sort of certification and must be registered with the Paramedics National Certification Registry, which typically requires a community college degree."

Rod Berens, President of Kingery Construction says, "Someone who works for us without a two-year degree in carpentry or construction management will earn about half as much in the first ten years as those with two-year degrees. Our carpenters and foremen who manage the construction site have at least a two-year degree in construction management. And any construction job is physical. We typically don't have older guys working on our crews. Those who want to work in the office and make even more have four-year construction management degrees."

Physical labor is dignified and noble work. But few bodies beyond age 55 can endure it daily. In fact, middle-aged workers rarely happily do jobs that require extended time standing. Get a two-year degree so that it's a much easier transition when your body tells you it's time for a good job that allows sitting.

LICENSES

Some careers do not require college degrees, but have their own training schools, such as cosmetology. This career attracts students annually in most high school graduation classes. To earn a license, a hair stylist typically needs about 18 months of beauty school costing about $20,000[93], an amount that does not include living expenses. So he or she can rack up about $30,000 in costs—often all borrowed money—to enter a field that can pay about $11 an hour plus tips. Ouch.

Many hair stylists by age 30 cite the paltry salary and standing all day as reasons for leaving. When I'm in the chair, I rarely see a hair stylist over the age of 30. But I get $20 haircuts. Cosmetologists can land in high-dollar salons and build up their clientele. These fortunate ones do earn better wages. But for the rest, changing careers is usually a sobering transition without a two- or four-year college degree, especially if you're looking for a good job that allows more sitting.

I encourage future beauty stylists to continue to work hard in high school so that they can quickly get a two-year degree in finance, business, or accounting before or during beauty school. Understanding business, despite the extra two years of time and expense, should make it more likely she can become a profitable salon owner someday rather than a low-income employee. If salon ownership is not on her radar, she has a solid college background with improved job prospects in the event she eventually chooses only to cut her friends' hair.

TRAINING PROGRAMS FOR HIGH SCHOOL GRADUATES

One participant told me that high school graduates with good scores on the Armed Services Vocational Aptitude Battery (ASVAB) are eligible for the Naval Nuclear Propulsion Program's two-year training program. Then after six to eight years, participants can qualify for six-figure, private sector jobs as nuclear technicians. He did say that the two years of training can be grueling (he quoted a 10 percent attrition rate) and then the subsequent lengthy stretches at sea can be especially so (he suggested that another 15 percent quit during tours.) Still, this can be a great pathway to a fine career without college and debt. Similar military options involving rigorous training for capable high school graduates also exist. Encourage students to ask the recruiter lots of questions.

MILITARY

Entering the military as infantry right out of high school is typically not a path to a good paying job, unless the student wants to be a lifetime military professional. A better option often is ROTC, which allows these future officers to attend college tuition-free, receive monthly stipends, and graduate before entering the military full time. The student has to commit to eight years of military service after graduation.[94] Fifteen percent of applicants win this prestigious, generous scholarship, an affordable pathway to leadership within the military and eventually as a civilian. Winning an ROTC scholarship usually requires at least a 24 on your ACT, a score often higher than what is required for admission to a specific college. Go to *rotc.military.com/rotc/program-browse.jsf* for a list of the hundreds of colleges that offer ROTC programs.

For the high school graduate not quite ready for college, the Coast Guard and Merchant Marine can also offer good training for a career in the military or law enforcement, good military benefits, and a safer military-related path before college or civilian life.

CIVIL AND COMMUNITY SERVICE

The website GoBankingRates.com in January 2015 listed ten other careers with decent average earnings potential that don't require college experience: waste-disposal personal ($25 an hour), sommelier ($28,000 a year with many earning much more), bingo manager ($59,000 a year), lodging manager ($56,000 a year), massage therapist ($40,000 a year), insurance agent ($63,000 a year), equipment operator ($41,000 a year), insurance claims adjuster ($62,000 a year), real estate broker ($53,000 a year), and telecom technician ($54,530).[95]

Still, many of these jobs are primarily sales jobs that require product expertise (sommelier, real estate broker, massage therapist, insurance agent).

The list of higher paying jobs not requiring a two- or four-year college diploma is short. Someday there may be meaningful job-related credentials available outside of colleges. We can always later add meaningful credentials and local job training programs to our primary Mission of creating two- and four-year graduates with minimal debt.

MARRY RICH

"Why don't you try?" I asked again, noticing that the hostile girl had not worked on the math questions I had just assigned.

She raised her eyes to me.

"I plan on marrying someone rich."

I smiled.

"Those who marry for money earn every penny."

Her changed expression momentarily suggested a reassessment of her approach.

FOR-PROFIT AND ONLINE COLLEGES

You may want to clarify whether the Mission should include any local for-profit or online colleges. Online education can lower the cost of college, but an exclusively online education denies the deep friendships and out-of-classroom learning possible when living and learning together.

After working as employees at different companies for a few years, three Virginia Tech fraternity brothers, Brian Callaghan, Win Sheridan, and Jeff Veatch, started their own staffing company in 1995. Seventeen years later, Apex Systems sold for $600 million.

Virginia Tech gave those three the ability to get good jobs right out of college and then the intuition to put that knowledge to work in their own company. Those four college years together also gave them a network of friends helpful in any career. If those three had earned online degrees, there probably never would have been an Apex Systems.

For-profit colleges educate about 10 percent of America's college students and create about 40 percent of the students delinquent on their student loan payments.[96] Fifty-five percent of their students drop out within a year.[97]

As of 2011, 13.7 percent of all student loan borrowers had defaulted within three years after they left school. At private colleges, 7.2 percent had defaulted within three years after leaving school. At public colleges 12.9 percent had defaulted. At for-profit colleges, 19.1 percent—one in five—had defaulted within three years.[98] For-profit colleges include Kaplan University, University of Phoenix, Strayer, DeVry, Vatterott, Capella, ITT, and others.

"Facing heavy losses and a crackdown by government agencies, Corinthian Colleges, one of the largest for-profit operators of trade schools and colleges, announced in July 2014 that it will largely cease operating. The California attorney general sued the company, charging, among other things, that it had lied to students and investors about job placement rates for its graduates and about its financial condition."[99]

"The predatory scheme devised by executives at Corinthian Colleges, Inc. is unconscionable. Designed to rake in profits and mislead investors, they targeted some of our state's most particularly vulnerable people—including low-income, single mothers and veterans returning from combat," the Attorney General said. "My office will continue our investigation into the for-profit college industry and will hold accountable those responsible for these illegal, exploitive practices."[100]

At for-profit colleges 19.1 percent—one in five students—had defaulted on their loans within three years.

The US Senate also has held many hearings on the for-profit college industry. Of course, bad apples don't spoil the entire bushel, but the curriculum offered at for-profit colleges is often readily available at non-profit, tax-payer subsidized community colleges for less money to the student.

SECTION 2 - HOW?

VI

HOW TO CREATE COLLEGE GRADUATES WITH MINIMAL DEBT (PART 1)

Job 1: Commit to the Expectation and Explain Why. "We create college graduates with minimal debt to improve our students' life chances in a demanding and hypercompetitive global economy."

Now how can we effectively accomplish it?

Job 2: Create a District-wide College-bound "Echo chamber."

With this clear and constant extrinsic motivation, the encouragement that it is a viable option for all, and a clear game plan for getting it done, more students will develop the internal drive to achieve that outcome.

HOW CAN WE TURN YOUR SCHOOL DISTRICT INTO A COLLEGE-BOUND ECHO CHAMBER?

It starts with the teachers and staff at every school, in every classroom from Kindergarten through twelfth grade. You are all now Assistant College Counselors.

Most teachers want to be well versed in the basics regarding how to get into the best college at the lowest cost, wanting to help and motivate their students, but also their own children. It breaks my heart when I hear that a teacher's own child over-spent for college. If there's a group of adults whose children deserve to win the college admissions game, it's hard-working teachers.

The Mission needs to start in elementary school, with the intensity growing through middle and high school. For example, a friend's complacent seventh grade son nearly accepted a demotion to a lower level math class. A caring teacher, though, told the father that going to the slower track would limit the future quality and breadth of math instruction the boy would experience in high school, probably affecting his college options. So the dad got involved, demanded the son stay in the accelerated math track, and explained why to his son. That suddenly more-motivated boy is now in eighth grade—and is a thriving A-student in his upper-level math class. Vague goals and implications create complacency. Clarity, communication, and vision create motivation.

The Mission needs to start in elementary school, with the intensity growing through middle and high school.

THE COUNSELORS: THE DRIVERS

Counselors are the logical choice for educating all staff members on the importance of graduating with minimal debt and how to get there, beginning with a presentation each year before the first day of school. Then, through brief presentations all year at each all-staff meeting and through social media and short videos, counselors can update the Mission effectively to staff, students, and parents. Counselors should present for at least five minutes to provide updates on college application and scholarship information every all-staff meeting. Teachers can chime in with their own and student-generated questions and observations.

Once teachers and administrators become informed evangelists, the counselor has dozens of daily allies spreading the word regarding scholarship deadlines, productive summer adventures, ROTC, the national merit scholarship, ACT (or SAT) test dates, taking the test four times, applying to at least seven colleges, and everything germane to every applicant's journey to a best-fit college at a low cost.

The goal is for everyone—not just staff and students, but also parents and community members—to become unified behind this message. Positive results then are less likely the result of serendipity or chance. And teachers are no longer islands within their own building but connected across disciplines in this coherent, common purpose.

HERE ARE THE BASICS THAT TEACHERS CAN EASILY MASTER AND SHARE.

The **annual** retail sticker price for college, everything included: room, board, fees, books, and tuition.

- Public universities (in-state residents): $13,000 (Peru State and Chadron State, NE) to $35,000 (U of Illinois, Vermont, and others)

- Public universities (non-residents): $13,000 (Peru State and Chadron State, NE) to $55,000 (University of Colorado, University of Michigan, University of Virginia, and others)

- Private colleges and universities: $25,000 to $70,000

Websites, newsletters, and 300-page books have been written on the secrets for getting into the right college at the right price. Their length and breadth can be daunting. The secrets to share with students can be synthesized down to ten simple thoughts—the Big Three plus the Next Seven.

The Big Three:

1. **GPA**: the combination of GPA and test scores is 90 percent of the battle.

    a. GPA often triggers the most generous public college scholarships for in-state residents. A class ranking in the top 10 percent helps most, but many big scholarships require just a top 25 percent class rank. A 3.5 GPA and a 32 ACT score triggers free tuition for four years at the University of Alabama (Tuscaloosa), reducing the annual net cost to about $12,000. A 3.0 GPA and a 33 ACT score triggers free tuition for four years at the University of Mississippi (Ole Miss at Oxford), also reducing the annual net cost to about $12,000.

    b. Grades 9, 10, 11, and the first semester of grade 12 are the grades that count. I recommend that schools have each student sign a pledge on the first day of each semester acknowledging that his GPA will affect his scholarships and cost for college. Then get his parents to sign it.

    c. Two or three Honors, Advanced Placement (AP), or International Baccalaureate (IB) classes a semester help. Rigor matters—it impresses admissions folks and makes college and adulthood easier. My AP classes not only made most of my Stanford classes seem easy, they have made many adult challenges seem comparatively manageable.

2. **Test Scores**:

a. Most of us only took the test once or twice, but with the rising cost of college, and knowing that the higher the score, the bigger the

> *Students should take the ACT or SAT three or four times.*

scholarships and the lower the cost, urge your students to take the ACT or SAT three or four times.

b. Colleges and scholarship committees typically just want to know the highest score. Many will 'super score' the test, using the best ACT sub-section scores from different tests to determine the overall ACT composite score. Nearly all colleges will 'super score' the SAT.

c. All colleges will accept either the ACT or SAT. The biggest difference between them is that the ACT has a Science Section. Students who loathe the science section, which actually primarily assesses comprehension of charts (not science), may want to sample the SAT. If a student has any question about her preferred test, she might try both by March of junior year so that she can easily take her preferred test three more times.

d. Students seeking admission to selective colleges or particularly competitive college scholarships may want to try 'the other test' in October or December of senior year to see if the needed score can be reached on that test.

e. Some selective schools will also ask for three SAT Subject Tests. Encourage students considering selective colleges to take three SAT Subject Tests right after taking the final in that subject—usually June of junior year.

f. Urge students to prepare each time they take a test. Taking sample tests or a proven, affordable test prep course makes a difference.

3. One extracurricular skill.

a. Athletic skills can trigger big scholarships, though college-level athletic skills often require considerable investment. Families will spend $5,000 a year and countless hours on club volleyball, but often won't prioritize studying, preparing for the ACT, or college application expertise. About 2 percent of high school seniors win college sports scholarships every year at NCAA institutions and the average amount is $11,000 total.[101] A 24 on the ACT combined with a 3.5 often results in at least $3,000 in scholarships a year in college.

b. Money invested in a child's brain development is money well spent. Low-cost summer camps can foster enthusiasm for science, math, art, or literature. Families will spend $300 on a prom dress but resist spending $300 for a week long science camp. Once parents and students realize that graduating from college with minimal debt is the true goal, better decisions get made.

c. Real skill in music, debate, chess, theatre, leadership, or an extracurricular beyond school (archery, FFA, etc.) can trigger scholarships and admissions acceptances. Quality, not quantity, matters more. Encourage students to prioritize.

d. Get them to market that skill— a "hello" email (to fifty softball coaches or jazz band directors) with a link to a ninety-second YouTube video of the applicant doing her skill and with a resume attached.

e. Coaches can help demystify and guide this process, while creating connections with college coaches for their current and future high school athletes. Though already overworked and underpaid, coaches and extracurricular leaders can be critical allies in this Mission to create college graduates with minimal debt.

f. If your counselors each have hundreds of students to help, your students may want additional personalized expertise. Either way, make sure your school's students can attack their college admissions journey to minimize regrets later.

The Next Seven:

1. Urge each student to **apply to 7 to 15 colleges**, including at least one school that fits the budget: a financial safety school.

   a. If Emma applies to a college, the only bad result can be a rejection or insufficient aid. No college will seize her dog or spray-paint her house.

b. A student who takes care of the Big Three but applies to merely one or two colleges effectively just fumbled inside the five-yard-line. Educators should advise against the *It-will-all-work-out* Approach:

　　i. Parents sometimes think that this critical college admissions journey will somehow all just work out because it worked out for them. But college was much less expensive when they went.

　　ii. Too many students and parents avoid "the Money Talk" until it's too late. The counseling staff at Crystal Lake South High School (Illinois) believes that too few students talk specifically about costs and budgets with parents until senior spring, when it's too late to add affordable colleges to the list. Consequently, too many applicants to four-year colleges wind up starting at two-year colleges. I'm a big fan of two-year degrees for vocational training (a two-year diesel mechanic degree can be

more valuable than a four-year communications degree), but for students seeking a four-year degree, those starting at a community college are less likely to get a four-year degree.[102] Further, those students will not have the deeper, richer experiences that four consecutive years at the four-year school could have allowed.

iii. Here's an all too common scenario.

1. Rachel has a 27 on her ACT, a 3.6 GPA, and a few solid extracurriculars at her Illinois high school. She gets gleaming acceptance letters. She soon learns that after scholarships, the net cost for Illinois State will be $26,000 a year, University of Illinois will be $33,000 a year, Marquette will be $35,000 a year, and University of Iowa will be $43,000 a year.

2. Rachel has two younger siblings. The family makes $140,000 a year, drives nice cars, and lives an upper-middle class lifestyle by all appearances. Perhaps they've even saved $10,000 in a College Savings Plan. Rachel can contribute about $10,000 a year to the cost of college by annually earning $5,000 and borrowing $5,000. Guess where Rachel will be attending school?

3. April brings rain and tears. Rachel in tearful disbelief finally gets the news from her parents that she'll be going to the local community

college because the family's true budget can't handle an additional $16,000 a year (plus pizza money).

iv. Too many students start at local community colleges rather than in a dorm and in the marching band at a four-year school because of this, *It-will-all-work-out* Approach. Teachers should join counselors urging the "Money Talk" in eighth grade—ninth grade at the latest.

v. Encourage each student to apply to at least seven strategically chosen schools—

1. Elite, highly selective schools that the family can afford or perhaps choose to borrow extra to attend (Northwestern, Yale, Swarthmore, etc.)

2. Solid schools with expected net costs within the budget—he'll probably get in and attend without over-borrowing (Doane, University of Alabama-Huntsville, Nebraska Wesleyan, Centre, Earlham, Montana Western, Missouri University of Science and Technology, in-state non-flagship public universities, University of North Dakota, University of Southern Arkansas, Central Michigan, Northwest Missouri State, Bemidji State, South Dakota School of the Mines, Hastings, Weber State, etc.) You might call these financial safety schools, but that title should not suggest any lack of quality: these schools offer very sound educations.

3. Money schools: colleges armed with merit-based aid so that the accomplished applicant gets a deep discount. Non-flagship public universities often deeply discount, especially for in-state residents or residents of nearby states that have reciprocal relationships with yours; see Appendix D in *College Common Sense: Get Into Your Best Fit College & Spend Less* for the colleges offering big merit-based scholarships (Washington & Lee, Emory, University of Mississippi, Brandeis, Denison, Ohio Wesleyan…).

vi. Bottom Line: urge them to apply to dream schools, but also to schools known for generous merit and need-based aid, and at least one college with a guaranteed low annual net cost that fits the family's budget. Every student needs a financial safety school or two on the list.

A girl in her senior year recently rejected Vassar for a full tuition scholarship at Nebraska Wesleyan. She is saving $50,000 a year so that her four siblings can receive more help from their parents for college. Plus Nebraska Wesleyan for $10,000 a year is a great education and value. Families must shop smart.

2. Urge your students to **apply for privately offered aid**: scholarships offered by private organizations. This money often goes not only to students armed with the Big Three, but also to students with less common skills and/ or well written short essays in response to the scholarship questions. Here are some free sites for finding privately-offered money.

> » FastAid.com

> » EducationQuest.org—or your state's equivalent

> » Your high school's web site—the counseling section should be a trove of local scholarships seeking worthy local kids. These local scholarships typically can be used only at in-state colleges.

3. Encourage your students to **work a job only on weekends and vacations**.

    a. Educators often surrender to this excuse for not doing the homework: "I had to work last night." If the culture is about creating college graduates with minimal debt, this excuse should only apply to students helping with the mortgage or the family food budget. The big money comes from the Big Three, which are compromised if too much time is spent on a low wage job. Working during high school can be valuable, but it can also be a distraction that brings little to the ultimate goal.

    b. Weekend and vacation work is fine because it acquaints students with the jobs that are available to those without college degrees. More motivation at school is a common result.

4. Encourage the parents to **visit with a financial advisor skilled in college finance**—one experienced with the FAFSA and how to maximize a family's eligibility for Need-Based Aid.

a. The FAFSA demonstrates a family's need-based aid eligibility; the money is often awarded first-come, first served. So urge seniors to submit the FAFSA between January 1 and January 15 of senior year of high school—and every year thereafter in college (FAFSA.gov). Finding local, retired financial experts to volunteer to help parents fill out their FAFSA can help ensure it gets done right.

b. Tell parents that they can fill out a practice FAFSA at FinAid.org.

c. Just submitting a FAFSA makes students eligible to borrow subsidized, lower-interest-rate loans.

Spending a year abroad as a foreign exchange student during high school or a "Gap Year" in a foreign country after high school usually makes a student a stronger college applicant.

5. Encourage eighth, ninth, and twelfth graders to **apply for a student-exchange year** attending high school and living with a host family in Paris, Montevideo, or elsewhere the following year: a gap year.

a. A student who spends freshman year, sophomore year, or the year after high school graduation (a gap year) in a foreign country matures quickly, becoming a stronger college applicant and a better prospect for graduation with minimal debt. One former student of mine told me he wanted to do a gap year in Spain so he could become bilingual and put on fifteen pounds of muscle. He would accept his best college offer but defer for a year. Then in Spain, he would contact other college football coaches to see if they'd have more interest because of his added bulk.

6. Applicants for selective colleges will also need **essays** and recommendations. These writing efforts often decide who gets in and who gets the scholarships. There are five keys to student-written essays and teacher recommendations:

    1. Be passionate about the topic.

    2. Less is more.

    3. Show; don't tell. It's the difference between writing, "I was angry." (tell) and "I flung the door open, stepped outside, and screamed." (show)

    4. Be specific.

    5. Add levity.

7. These five apply to teacher **recommendations** as well. Vague platitudes about the student's congeniality and

---

On letters of recommendation, vague platitudes about a student's congeniality and wisdom won't help. Specifics will.

---

wisdom won't help. Specifics will. Colleges recognize form letters. Recommendation letters affect admissions and scholarships. A recommendation-writing workshop for high school teachers before each year would serve your students and the Mission.

That's it. The Big Three plus the Next Seven can become sources of celebration—or sources of regret for seniors who learn them too late. College counselors know this list. Other staff members need just a basic understanding of the Big Three and the Next Seven so together they can amplify the *Reaching Higher* Mission early and often during your students' Kindergarten through twelfth grade journey:

1. College is increasingly important because of intelligent machines and inexpensive foreign labor—valuable skills and knowledge matter in the face of these unrelenting global forces,

2. The Big Three, the Next Seven, and specifics on popular colleges and their scholarships can lower the cost.

MERIT-BASED AID AND NEED-BASED AID

Colleges award financial aid—grants, scholarships, loans, and work study—based on merit and/or need. Grants and scholarships are free money. Loans are part of the net cost, but will be paid later with interest.

The Big Three—GPA, scores, and one extracurricular—trigger merit-based aid.

A family's financial wherewithal determines need. Each family in early January should fill out the FAFSA found at FAFSA.gov. Within days, they should receive their EFC: Expected Family Contribution. The lower the EFC, the better.

But the Big Three also dictate the size and composition of need-based aid. If Sophia barely meets the admissions requirements, that college is unlikely to satisfy all of her need, and Sophia can expect her aid offer to include a hefty loan. If Sophia's merit makes her coveted by college admissions committees, her need-based aid offers should not only be near the allowed maximum (based on her EFC), but her need-based aid offers should also primarily be grants and scholarships—free money—rather than loans. The Big Three affect both merit-based aid and the composition and amount of need-based aid.

I will never forget that boy loudly asking: "Why didn't they tell us this? I didn't know any of this."

So any unmotivated lower-income student is either unaware of his eligibility for need-based aid or a masochist, engaged in self-sabotage. A student from a family making less than $70,000 a year should qualify for ample need-based aid. By not putting forth the needed effort in school, he denies himself the best opportunity he may ever have to climb the economic ladder.

Educators should figuratively grab all unmotivated lower income students by their collars, starting in Kindergarten and continuing through graduation, to explain the upward mobility associated with college graduation and how lower income means that even nominal academic merit can trigger maximum need-based aid, leading to a degree with minimal debt.

Low-income students that don't work hard simply break my heart. I'm convinced from first-hand experience that a huge percentage would alter their approach if they just knew at a young age about education's impact. I will never forget that boy loudly asking: "Why didn't they tell us this? I didn't know any of this!"

Now that we know the Why and the How, what further can we do verbally and visibly to create this College-Bound Echo Chamber, turning our schools into college prep schools that create future two- and four-year college graduates with minimal debt?

THE MONEY TALK

Encourage students to discuss the family's college budget early during high school. Long-time suburban Chicago counselor Pat Olsen-McGee has many stories that prove the importance of the Money Talk.

"The most common family story is this one, and it drove me crazy. Students would say they wanted to go to Iowa, Michigan, Wisconsin, Valparaiso, Purdue, Notre Dame, or some other well-known big university. My question—to both students and parents—was what is your **financial "safety school?"**

"We do not have one. We will just find scholarships if he gets in."

So he gets in! And the costs vary from over $20,000 to $45,000 at each school. They start working on 'scholarships' in March! Then they come into my office soon after this 'search.'

"We cannot afford any of these schools. What do we do?"

"Well there's not a lot that can be done at this point because merit scholarships have a DEADLINE. Many of these four-year college students had to start at community college or over-borrow simply because there had never been an honest Money

Talk about the typical net cost for each college on the list and the family's true capacity to pay it—sad, sad story, over and over and over again."

Pat continues, "During my first year of counseling, I watched a competition for a local $1,000 scholarship. One of the citizens awarding the money asked one of our seniors how he would pay for his college, Drake University, which at the time cost about $27,000 a year. His reply was 'My parents are taking out a second mortgage on our house.' I almost had a stroke. He had had a C average in high school. The cost combined with his lack of study skills landed him back home—at least $20,000 in debt after just one year. All of this could have been avoided with an honest Money Talk, a cap on annual debt, and serious consideration of comparable colleges with lower price tags."

That high school did everything right except ensuring that every one of its families knew the critical importance of becoming a college graduate with minimal debt.

"One family did get it. They took their daughter to Iowa City, where the University of Iowa offered her a $5,000 scholarship that very day. The dad asked his daughter on the way home where she wanted to visit next and suggested some less costly schools: UW-Parkside, Central Michigan, and a few others. She replied, 'I do not want to visit any other schools. I am going to Iowa. They are giving me a scholarship.'

"He tells her that $5,000 is like a 10 percent off coupon and that they could not afford Iowa. Both parents were unwilling to go into significant debt when comparable college options existed at much lower price points.

"So the daughter becomes surly. She would not look at other schools, despite multiple talks with her counselor and her parents. She ended up at the local community college, where she matured, did well, and transferred to a four-year college, where she is very successful.

"That girl could have earned a much lower net cost at a 'lesser' four-year school, but she wouldn't listen after seeing a school that she only learned after the fact was out of her price range."

Moral: parents should have the Money Talk long before visiting the Mercedes Dealer. In fact, there are plenty of Mercedes-quality vehicles on the used Chevy lot. Most vehicles, if driven well, can get you to the same destination. Teachers can help counselors send both messages.

A PROVEN PATHWAY TO
SKILLS AND KNOWLEDGE
A TWO- OR FOUR-YEAR COLLEGE DEGREE
WITH MINIMAL (OR NO) DEBT!

VII

HOW TO CREATE COLLEGE GRADUATES WITH MINIMAL DEBT (PART 2)

Teachers and administrative staff, our front line, are now assistant college counselors, sharing the Mission verbally and visibly.

1. **Communicate specifics on Intelligent Machines, Globalization, and the Big Three: GPA, Scores, and One Extracurricular.**

It's a simple message. Intelligent Machines and Inexpensive Foreign Workers advance every day. Real skills and knowledge compete against them effectively. A two- or four-year college degree with minimal debt is a proven path to critical, differentiating, empowering skills and knowledge. A casual approach to learning now will likely lead to economic struggles later.

College is pricey. Taking care of the Big Three—GPA, test scores, and one extracurricular—will yield merit-and need-based aid. At their five-year high school reunion, everyone can be a college graduate with minimal debt.

2. Offer dual credit courses and mandate that students take the AP test at the end of each AP course taken.

Students at many high schools can stockpile a semester or even year of college credit, lessening the time and cost to graduate. Dual credit classes visibly embody the Mission and increase its likelihood. Taking an AP test costs about $100, but if mandated, makes all AP students more serious. Once on board with the Mission, local boosters might have an interest in sharing some of the costs for taking AP tests. A score of 4 or 5 on an AP test means college credit and an impressive addition to any scholarship or college application.

Encourage your successful students to take an AP test even if they haven't been in an AP class. For example, a successful student in a regular biology class with a little preparation in an AP Biology Prep book might do well on the AP Biology test.

3. Communicate regularly with thriving local businesses to ensure that your Mission and curriculum teach the skills they seek.

    a.   If the local economy needs more welders, and few local economies don't, make sure that students know this, know the eventual salary expectations, have the basic math to pass the college welding classes, and understand the path to get that career.

4. Hang that College Diploma on your classroom wall.

I don't tell my dentist how to handle my teeth. Yet some parents tell teachers how to teach. Hang that diploma in a prominent space with soft lighting aimed on it—and gaze upon it when some obnoxious parent tries to bully you.

5. Promote summer experiences in your discipline.

The basketball coach doesn't tell her players in June, "Hey, I'll see you in the fall." No. Teams work through the summer to hone and develop their skills. The science department can cultivate the same mentality. Promote summer science experiences and science camps. Here's how.

Google "summer science camps for high school students within a hundred miles." Contact the camp directors and tell them you want students from your school attending each summer. With the information the camps provide, you can put together quick snapshot summaries of each camp: cost, how scholarships can be applied for, deadlines. Then, post each summary online for students and parents. Prominently post paper versions on your classroom walls. Then, as deadlines approach, write on the board the name of the camp and application deadline, and ask who is applying.

If an essay is required to apply, perhaps assign that essay as homework in your class. If just three students in each of your science classes attend a science camp for a week in the summer, those kids will return as more interested, confident, and worldly students. Soon others will want the same experience.

Parents can be overwhelmed, unsure how to create productive summers for their children. Often these camps are not expensive, and some have scholarship opportunities for low-income families. Transportation can also be an issue, but talk to the Camp Directors for alternatives. If teachers have answers for the possible objections, it keeps barriers from being erected where they don't need to be. All departments—math, industrial arts, English, social studies, visual and performing arts—can advocate for summer programs. Coordinate with your college counselor(s) and your department colleagues to promote productive experiences in your subject area, transforming your students and their passions for your subject. Fight the summer slide!

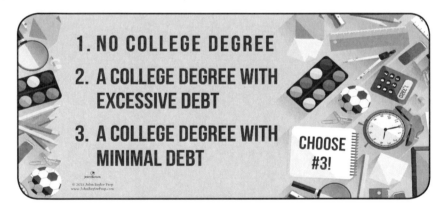

6. Other related messages to share:

Explain the three outcomes and have students choose their intended destination. Will it be no college degree, a college degree with excessive debt, or a college degree with minimal to zero debt? A sign on your classroom wall with the three outcomes would be a nice daily reminder.

√ Promote the basics for getting into the best college at the lowest cost (see the Big Three and the Next Seven).

Fight the "summer slide" by promoting productive summer experiences in your subject area.

√ Encourage juniors to prepare for and take at least two ACTs or two SATs before senior year—I often see big score jumps on the June test because most students have fewer distractions then.

√ Encourage seniors to prepare for and take at least two ACTs or two SATs before January—the December test is typically the last one that counts for financial aid.

√ Master and share the scholarship basics for the top six local colleges where the bulk of your graduates attend: retail sticker price, scholarship dates, what's required, etc.

√ Ask your students what skills they'll be building over the summer.

√ Show them the JBP *Become a Two- or Four-year Grad with Minimal Debt* speech on JohnBaylorPrep.com— just click on JBP Public Vignettes.

√ Caution students against borrowing more than $5,000 a year. (Future engineers can borrow more, while future artists might borrow less.) $20,000 total in debt can be paid off over nine years for about $215 a month.

√ Tell your stories, good and bad, from your own, your children's, and your past students' college experiences. Your students and their parents crave specifics.

√ Ask administrators to provide each student with an advisor, a teacher connected with that student. Advisors can personally share the *Reaching Higher* Mission and help during difficult times. A formal advisor can be one more critical adult relationship for each student. I know that my advisor was critical.

√ Four thousand high schools have students apply to college while in class.[103] This strategy can especially help your low-income students get the job done.

√ Make sure all jocks at the beginning of ninth grade know how important academics are if they wish to play college sports. New 2015 NCAA eligibility rules require high school athletes to have a GPA of at least 2.3 in 16 core courses (up from 2.0 and 13 core courses). And ten of those courses must be completed in the first three years of high school to be eligible to compete as a college freshman. Once a student completes a course in his or her first three years, that course cannot be retaken for a better grade. Ninth grade counts!

7. **Have fun with the Mission. Make learning and the conquest of college cool.**

The Mission should be visible as well as verbal.

√ Create display cases featuring photos of recent grads: "Thanks Mr. Jones for inspiring me to love chemistry. I'll be graduating from Bemidji State next year with less than $10,000 in debt! Ka-boom!"

√ Create Banners like these:

> » "Don't be a wimp. Take the ACT 4 times."
>
> » "Commit to being a 24-year-old college grad with minimal debt!"
>
> » "Only wimps pay full price for college!"
>
> » "Have the Money Talk with your family NOW! Love, Your Lovable Counselors."
>
> » The school's last five years of ACT scores and the percentage taking the test
>
> » A list of five favorite well-known colleges and their retail sticker price

√ List Seniors next to their colleges; put this list on a huge School Banner, the Graduation Program, the local paper, the school paper, and a poster that you give to local vendors to display in their store front windows. Let the town become part of your echo chamber.

√ After each graduation, hang up the new banner prominently in school and move the old one to the cafeteria, which soon will be lined with these banners of the names of graduates from prior years and the colleges they planned to graduate from.

√ Display pennants from colleges attended by last year's class.

√ List each name from last year's graduating class under the pennant of the college he or she is attending. [104] [105] [106] [107]

Last Year's Graduates: Where Are They Now?			
Drew, Nancy	Bennett, Elizabeth	Finn, Huckleberry	Baggins, Frodo
Holmes, Sherlock	Butler, Rhett	Shirley, Anne	Eyre, Jane
Pevensie, Lucy	Dantes, Edmond	Pan, Peter	
Sawyer, Tom	Ingalls, Laura		
Twist, Oliver			

√ Make scholarship and other college admissions announcements whenever many are present—halftimes, intermissions, school concerts, sporting events.

√ Turn counselors into movie stars, communicating scholarship and admissions specifics. How? Produce four-minute videos on these germane topics:

VIDEO: Why our Mission is to create two- and four-year college graduates with minimal debt

VIDEO: ROTC versus entering the military right out of high school

VIDEO: Why all students with a top 10 percent class rank must prepare for and take the October junior year PSAT.

Example: I know a student, who ultimately scored a perfect 36 on his ACT, but did not take the PSAT in October of his junior year, 2013. Yikes. That oversight cost his family thousands in National Merit money he surely would have won. All students with a shot at a National Merit scholarship should take the October, junior year PSAT! Any strong student with a 170 or higher on a sophomore year PSAT is a prospect.

VIDEO: How to visit colleges, why, and when (see *College Common Sense: Get Into Your Best Fit College & Spend Less*).

VIDEO: How Selective College admissions differ: essays and recommendations (the final two). How to ask and thank teachers for recommendations (It is customary for a student to write hand-written thank you notes—after the recommendations are sent).

VIDEO: Mistakes made and successes from last five graduating classes.

VIDEO: What are the skills most in demand in the local area? How do you get this skill, and what do these jobs pay. Every seventh grader should know what these local technical jobs pay and the skills they require.

Example: A welding degree from community college typically reaps a starting salary of $35,000 or higher. How many adrift students could be hooked just by knowing how lucrative certain vocations are?

"The average age of welders is 54, and the American Welding Institute predicts openings for more than 400,000 welders by 2024. In the burgeoning shale industry, in Texas and Appalachia, welders can earn as much as $7,000 a week."[108]

√ First Day of School Each Year: Present the College Message with staff, teachers and administrators all involved (or show the JBP *Become a Two- or four-year College Grad with Minimal Debt* speech at JohnBaylorPrep.com) Parents should see the presentation that same day via email. This will spur healthy conversations that week at home! The parents have to get the Mission so that they, too, become teacher allies.

√   Create a senior celebration. Here are some examples:

Example: Platteview High School brings the entire seventh grade through twelfth grade population into the auditorium on a school day in the spring. Rock music plays while each senior comes forward for a t-shirt from his or her future college. The screen behind shows that student's future college and scholarships. Video messages from recent graduates about how much they love college play on the screen. Educators toss out college gear, donated by local colleges. Underclassmen get the Mission.

Example: Crystal Lake South High School has a senior signing day. Every senior signs a congratulatory certificate, declaring their next college or career choice--similar to the signing ceremony for future college athletes. Photos from the ceremony in the gym land on the school's web site, where thousands of hits result. Underclassmen and parents get the message.

Example: Have recent graduates return to tell their stories about college (at least on video if not in person), reviewing the mistakes they made—not visiting enough colleges, delaying the "Money Talk" with parents, thinking that scholarships would just materialize, only taking the ACT or SAT twice, not preparing for the test, only applying to three schools, not learning during the summer slide, not leaning on mentors from high school or college, and so on. Post these edited videos on the school's web site.

√   Educate your students on how to avoid three common mistakes—applying to only one or two colleges, taking the ACT only once or twice, and having the Money Talk too late.

VIII

POST-HIGH SCHOOL EFFORT
TO MAXIMIZE THE LIKELIHOOD
OF GRADUATION

The work to inform all students about how to go to their best fit college at the lowest cost must be done prior to high school graduation. But a high school's effort to turn all seniors into college graduates with minimal debt should continue beyond high school graduation.

I just lost all high school educators.

Teaching your current students is all consuming. Continuing to guide recent graduates may seem impossible. However, minimal effort, through email and social media, can ensure all this current effort reaps the intended outcome: two- and four-year college graduates with minimal debt.

Counselors tell me that too many students change their mind during that summer right after high school graduation and don't enroll in college that fall. In fact, academic studies estimate that 10 to 40 percent of recent high school graduates intending to start college that fall, don't do so. The percentages are much higher for low-income and first generation college students.[109]

Whether it's the summer after graduation or the years after, continued connections with recent graduates can avert disastrous decisions. I remember learning that two high school basketball stars had quit college in their second year. I asked their high school coach what he had done to try to change their minds. He said he had maintained no contact with them. These were two former state champion athletes who made this life-changing choice without even consulting their former coach of four years.

Here's how to guide your recent high school graduates with minimal effort.

- Each high school staff member chooses a group of his favorite seniors to email each month for the next four years. A counselor or teacher writes twelve interesting emails about the happenings at school—one for each month. The first week of each month, beginning in June, each teacher personalizes that message and emails it to his chosen former students (and perhaps their parents as well).

- A close high school teacher often knows the student more than any other adult outside the family. In a new college environment, your former students need advisors more than ever. Too often they'll make life-changing decisions with minimal guidance. I know that I did back then. These monthly messages will remind them that you're still there.

- Use these monthly emails to encourage them to seek out professors and free student tutors, to go to the library daily, to graduate on time (in two or four years), to pursue their productive passions (including an extracurricular), to make a lot of money during vacations, to borrow no more than $20,000 total, and to find new mentors. Graduating takes work—and sometimes a village. Dr. Shane Lopez says that one indicator of college success is the number of older people on campus that the student knows. With age usually comes wisdom.

- Further, if any graduate makes it big, you'll want to have some history of regular contact when you ask for that huge donation for your school's Foundation.

Monthly emails during those key years right after high school can reduce the chance of impetuous, regrettable choices undoing thirteen years of effort.

- These regular monthly contacts can continue advisor-student friendships into adulthood and increase the likelihood that Billy graduates rather than drops out. Monthly emails during those key years right after high school can reduce the chance of impetuous, regrettable choices undoing thirteen years of effort. And parents at odds with their 20-year-old will be so grateful that you're still there to help and persuade.

And this next section is critical:

HAVE YOUR HIGH SCHOOL TRACK COLLEGE GRADUATION RATES THROUGH THE NATIONAL CLEARINGHOUSE.[110]

The college graduation rate does not change much after six years following high school. I have asked many high school staffs if

they remember the class that graduated six years prior. Many nod. I'll then ask if they'd like to know what percentage of that class has earned a two- or four-year degree. They all say yes. They also say they have no idea what the percentages are.

Once a school embraces the Mission, college graduation with minimal debt for every student—from Kindergarten through twelfth grade—this college graduation percentage becomes central. Teachers instinctively know that the school's six-year college graduation rate affects lives, that it actually may be a valid measure of their work. Use the National Clearinghouse to track your two- and four-year college graduation rate. What gets measured gets done.

Tracking the average debt upon graduation for your two- and four-year graduates might be more difficult, but perhaps they'll tell you if you keep in touch during college through monthly emails.

And much can be done to drive home the Mission during senior spring, that final semester before college. Counselors need to be intimately involved in each senior's ultimate college choice. I wish my counselor had been. Any senior choosing a more expensive option is more vulnerable to dropping out.

Counselors can also help families negotiate financial aid offers. Those initial aid offers often can be increased thanks to shrewd negotiations that leverage lower net costs at comparable colleges.

Senior spring can also be a time to amplify the message that academic and social struggles may lurk in college but are temporary. Steve Koch, principal at Prairie Ridge High School in Illinois agrees. "We bring in a panel of college freshmen and sophomores to talk to seniors about the transition to college. Our students are attentive to their every word!"

Bill Gates writes, "The problem isn't that not enough people are going to college. The problem is that not enough people are finishing."[111]

IX

BOLSTER THE MISSION BY PUSHING ALL STUDENTS TO GET MORE THAN THE DEGREE: GET AN EDUCATION

Debuting in 2014, the movie *Ivory Tower* is about the costs, results, and future of conventional four-year residential colleges. At one point, the audience hears a recording of a television anchor ominously declaring "nearly half of all students are showing no significant gains in learning."[112]

The source of that data is the book *Academically Adrift*, authored in 2010 by Richard Arum and Josipa Roksa, which cites that 45 percent of students demonstrate no significant improvement in a range of skills—including critical thinking, complex reasoning, and writing—during their first two years of college.

"Thirty-six percent of the kids in our study say they studied less than five hours a week, less than an hour a day—full time college students! Half the kids in our study said they didn't have a single class where they wrote more than twenty pages."[113]

"Arum and Roksa argue that this data is the result of a student body distracted by socializing or working, and an institutional culture that puts undergraduate learning close to the bottom of the priority list."[114]

So adult romper room educations are available and can render that college degree worth not much more than a ticket to job interviews. Getting and keeping a good job will be unlikely for the students who join the many others doing so little.

A four- to five-year beverage fest is incongruent with true education. A degree alone can lead to interviews and some job offers. But an actual education inculcates critical reasoning, grit, and deeper thinking, so often cornerstones of successful adulthoods. Without the college graduation with minimal debt expectation, it's unlikely high school students will hear much about the distinction between a mere degree and an engaging education delving in productive passions.

Once your students scatter, they can make impulsive decisions. There are practical, time-tested strategies for increasing the likelihood for a degree and an education. Share your own dos and dont's before your seniors leave. Your students crave honesty. Here's our list for How to Maximize College so that they graduate, joining the 55 percent who start and actually finish college (You can also play the video *How To Maximize College,* found under *College Counseling* in JohnBaylorPrep.com.).

- **Students should live on campus.** I've never understood the excitement over living off campus. They have the rest of their lives to live off campus. Very few people my age live in dorms. Let others bicker over utility bills and dishes. On-campus housing may be more expensive than off-campus, but jeopardizing graduation chances can be truly pricey.

- **Urge students to leave their car at home.** Many students have cars in high school because very few live at high school. However, they'll be living on campus in college. Where are they going? Encourage them to find a college within biking

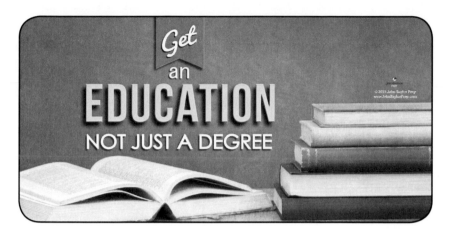

distance of that destination. Leaving the car at home saves nearly enough to pay for the premium cost of living on campus. Plus they have four-plus months of vacation time each year to drive.

- **Urge them to get a bike.** Haven't they heard of the Freshman Fifteen? They need a bike.

- **Students should meaningfully participate in one extracurricular skill**. Members of the marching band, jazz band, volleyball team, and theater casts rarely drop out of college. Those more likely to drop out live off-campus with their high school buddies, drive to school, and work an off-campus job twenty hours a week to pay for the car. All these small decisions together compromise the college experience and make graduation less likely. Encourage them to live on campus, to get a bike, and to participate meaningfully in one extracurricular. Hello graduation!

- **Students should try to take only small classes. Writing, reading, and speaking skills are critical.** Future influence requires strong communication prowess. Large lazy lecture halls rarely teach strong communication skills. Students should take small scintillating seminar classes whenever possible—or they can make themselves accountable by sitting in the front of every class and participating regularly. By honing reading, writing, and speaking skills, sitting in the front of class, and being accountable, students should nail their job interviews and become more influential and successful adults.

> » <u>A note regarding the Humanities</u>. Science, technology, engineering, and math (STEM) majors are statistically the best way to financial success early in a career. But majoring in humanities teaches the ability to think critically; research shows that liberal arts majors may not be compensated as much short term but make up for it over time.[115] Companies may not pay for knowledge of American Literature or Latin, but they will pay over time for the cerebral capacity necessary to master them—a capacity often greater than what business requires.

- **Students should choose college classes with great teachers only.** Students can find great teachers through the many student blogs critiquing professors. Highly skilled, passionate teachers and lousy, lazy teachers inhabit most campuses. Your students should only take classes taught by great professors.

- **Students can and should master another language**. Your students can be bilingual—to enrich their job prospects and lives. Spanish is simple to learn, compared to most languages. Spanish skill will dramatically enhance job applications and job security in many professions. Mandarin, Arabic, and Russian are also practical, though much more difficult to master. A semester abroad won't do it. Two semesters should get them closer.

- **Students should work no more than ten hours per week during college.** Nearly one-out-of-five full-time college students in this country works 35 hours a week or more.[116] Although sometimes necessary, this level of job commitment compromises the college experience. If feasible, students should work ten, at most 15 hours a week during the weeks of college and 45 to 75 hours a week during vacations.

- **Students should borrow no more than $20,000 total by graduation.** We don't want students making more than $250 monthly loan payments in their twenties, nor any payments in their thirties. So about $5,000 a year, or $20,000 total, puts them at about $215 a month until age thirty-one. Engineers should feel free to borrow more, while aspiring artists might borrow less. (And if they're on a budget and want to study art, they can go to Chadron State or Peru State in Nebraska or Weber State in Utah for about $13,000 total a year or to an art school in Canada for less than $22,000 a year.) The last thing an artist needs is significant debt.

- **Students should take at least one semester each of Accounting, Finance, Math, Science, US Social History, and Art History.** These courses will improve their chances of being a business owner, help them understand money, sharpen their minds, enhance their understanding of topics shaping economic and political trends, and deepen their appreciation for life and art.

- **Urge students to find their next mentor(s) soon after they arrive on campus**.

- **Encourage students to gravitate towards their productive passions**. Too many people are guided by "supposed to's." Adulthood is filled with compromise and supposed to's, largely because we have children and other responsibilities. Adolescence is a time to chase big dreams relatively free from compromise and "supposed to's." There are too many achievement-oriented, credential-consumed, affluent youths angling their choices towards the impressive rather than the personally important; they are "accomplishment hoarders" in the quest to land an elite college. College should be about grasping an actual education, filled with productive passions rather than simply a degree.

X

ADMINISTRATOR RESPONSIBILITIES CREATED BY THE *REACHING HIGHER* MISSION

It would take courage for Administrators and School Board members to champion a new Mission that creates the expectation that every K-12 student can and will graduate from college with less than $20,000 in debt. Though inexpensive to implement and potentially transformative for all constituents, this Mission creates more responsibilities for those at the top.

Since our communities currently emphasize high school graduation, most K-12 school leaders view high school graduation as the ultimate goal and thus, their final responsibility in their students' journey. Some private high schools and mainly affluent public high schools may publicize their seniors' college destinations, announcing and tracking the numbers and percentages of seniors starting in selective colleges, local colleges, community colleges, the work force, and military. That's usually it.

Embracing and selling the Mission to faculty, staff, students, parents, and community members adds to a Superintendent's or High School Principal's typical responsibilities. Tracking two- and four-year college graduation rates through the National Clearinghouse is one such example. There are a few additional tasks that will be critical as well.

One would involve a thorough understanding of how colleges treat recent graduates. When I ask superintendents or high school principals what percentage of their graduates takes remedial classes, they typically cannot tell me. They've never been asked.

A community college representative admitted to me that about 50 percent of their full-time first year students are taking at least one remedial class. I asked him how superintendents respond to that. He told me that he's rarely been asked. When speaking to high school students, I typically have to explain what remedial classes in college are: high school do-over classes that cost money, result in no college credits, increase the cost and time required for the degree, and decrease the likelihood of graduation.

"Students in remedial reading or math have particularly dismal chances of success. A US Department of Education study found that 58 percent of students who do not require remediation earn a bachelor's degree, compared to only 17 percent of students enrolled in remedial reading and 27 percent of students enrolled in remedial math."[117]

"When considering all first-time undergraduates, studies have found anywhere from 28 percent to 40 percent of students enroll in at least one remedial course. When looking at only community college students, several studies have found remediation rates surpassing 50 percent. Forty-one percent of Hispanic students and 42 percent of African-American students require remediation, compared to 31 percent of white students."[118]

"Strong American Schools estimates the costs of remedial education to states and students at around $2.3 billion each year. Compounding the costs is the fact that remedial students are more likely to drop out of college without a degree. Less than 25 percent of remedial students at community colleges earn a certificate or degree within eight years."[119]

Lowering remediation rates will save money. "The Alliance for Excellent Education suggests that reducing the need for remediation could generate an extra $3.7 billion annually from decreased spending on the delivery of remedial education and increased tax revenue from students who graduate with a bachelor's degree."[120]

You get the idea.

I've heard many stories of recent graduates retaking high school courses at the local college despite a decent high school grade in that course. Perhaps they didn't prepare for or take seriously the college's placement tests that dictated which course they could take initially. Perhaps they just need to prepare for and take those placement tests during their senior year of high school, before amnesia sets in. Perhaps the local college did not sufficiently respect high school grades.

High school leaders focused on college graduation can help repair this problem by having seniors prepare for and take the ACT. Preparing for and taking the Compass, or other Community College placement tests, will then be comparatively simple. To minimize remedial classes, high school administrators can also defend their recent graduates in communications with local college leaders. A school district focused on its students' overarching interest in a college degree with minimal debt will monitor the remediation rate of its graduates and seek solutions.

Superintendents who embrace the new Mission for America's schools might also vet and rate the training programs offered by local companies for new hires. The better ones might be promoted as skill-building alternatives to college.

CONCLUSION

Test scores stress educators. But test scores are symptoms. If school is cool, it's cool to be smart. It's cool to hammer the grammar. It's cool to talk about colleges. It's cool to visit colleges. It's cool to get letters from colleges. It's cool to be applying to a lot of colleges. It's even cool to take the ACT or SAT—countless students throw on our Hammer the Grammar t-shirts and eye-black on test day. If we can just hook more kids by communicating the Mission, the symptoms improve: test scores, truancy, tardiness, cell phone distractions, bullying, and extracurricular involvement.

Trent Linbo was bright but bored, distracting himself into a few Bs and Cs in ninth grade. He later learned that grades affected scholarships. He eventually earned a hefty 34 on his ACT. He

Attack the cause, and you'll reduce the symptoms.

wanted to attend the local state university, where he later excelled in chemical engineering. But those early Bs and Cs tumbled his class rank below the top 10 percent, costing him a full tuition scholarship: $34,000 in free tuition over four years. If he had just known that ninth grade classes affected his future scholarships, he would've been focused in school. No one told him. Or if they did tell him, they didn't make sure he was listening.

A small town senior told me he already had a 29 on his ACT, the highest in his class, and that he didn't want to take the test again. "A 29 is the precipice of big scholarships," I told him. He took the JBP online ACT Prep course and jumped his score to a 34. But he still missed out on $34,000 in free tuition—again because of some earlier low grades that kept his class rank below the top ten percent. That's $34,000 he had to borrow and pay back during his twenties and thirties because no one told him how all high school grades and scores affected college costs.

A senior told me he wanted to go into the military. "What about ROTC?" I asked. He looked at me and asked, "What exactly is ROTC?"

"ROTC is a program that pays your college tuition and leads to a much safer and better paying job as an officer." Unless they learn about ROTC freshman year, upper-classmen headed to the military sometimes have made academic choices that jeopardize their ability to win an ROTC scholarship. If he had known about ROTC earlier, he may have exerted himself in high school. His parents probably would've been a lot happier as well.

"I want to be a bartender," a girl told me in class.

"Terrific. But what if you get fired, or get tired of standing at work, or want to make more money, or want a different profession? What if technology allows bars to go self-serve and the demand for bartenders shrinks?" If she had heard a similar, coordinated message since ninth grade, those teachers may have seen more effort from her. Bartending can be a fine, fun profession, though rarely one pursued full-time for life. Having at least a two-year degree can make a later change of heart less difficult.

IMPROVING ACADEMIC OUTCOMES

Instead of attacking apathy and motivating more kids with the *Reaching Higher* Mission, educators currently are asked to focus on tests themselves. The Partnership for Assessment of Readiness for College and Careers (**PARCC**) test has consumed immeasurable energy within our nation's school buildings. Administrators and educators have sat through hours of meetings regarding how it will be rolled out. In my latest trip to Chicago-area high schools, educators expressed frustration with and criticism for the process. Imagine if they had spent merely a fraction of that time developing their school's plan for creating more college graduates with minimal debt.

Here was the breakdown for the Marengo, Illinois, High School Class of 2011: 47 percent to a four-year school, 37 percent to a two-year school, 11 percent to work, 3 percent to military, and 2 percent unsure.

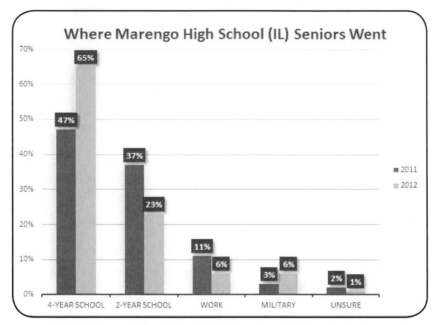

Marengo High in Illinois has about 200 seniors each year. In just one year, its college-going rate went from 84 percent to 88 percent, with the four-year college-going rate climbing from 47 percent to 65 percent of all seniors.

One year later, here was the breakdown for Marengo's Class of 2012: 65 percent to a four-year school, 23 percent to a two-year school, 6 percent to work, 5 percent to military and 1 percent unsure. In one year the college-going rate went from 84 percent to 88 percent, with the 4-year college enrollment rate jumping from 47 percent to 65 percent. How did Marengo do it? A dedicated faculty and an invigorated culture emphasized going to the best, most affordable college and graduating with minimal debt.

Students encouraged one another to take the ACT test during their junior and senior years. They prepared hard for a test that actually served the Mission and applied to lots of colleges.

At a softball game one May afternoon, the Marengo team discovered that their ACT scores had come out that day. Players asked each other their scores while they checked their phones to learn their own.

One Marengo teacher emailed his Principal: "I was talking to Jess today, and she was telling me how mad she was that Torbin was posting on Facebook that this year's ACT must have been easier because there were so many 30's this year. She truly was ticked about it...Awesome!" Enthusiasm breeds results.

We can ignite an enthusiasm for learning that lies dormant in too many young people. We can ignite our school culture. Connecting the dots—explaining how intelligent machines and inexpensive foreign labor make school more important—creates motivation. We can regularly share the specifics for how to get a best-fit college at a low cost. And such an environment should foster a Growth Mindset in all our students.

Eighty percent of our students' waking hours during their K-12 years are spent outside of school. We lament the distractions beyond our control that undermine their learning. But we can hook kids with a clear message. We can go on offense, armed with a Mission to create college graduates with minimal debt, converting apathetic students and parents. More enthusiastic students, happier teachers, stronger graduates, and stronger communities await.

The world has dramatically changed. Let's use that as motivation. I've seen it work. Let's do it.

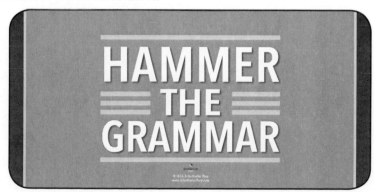

The Eight-Week Schedule for Effectively Implementing the Strategy

Week one:

1. Principals, Superintendent, and School Board:

    a. Decide with K-12 Staff Leaders and counselors that you wish to implement the new *Reaching Higher* Mission: "We Create Two- and Four-Year College Graduates with Minimal Debt."

    b. Get buy-in from staff leaders and counselors.

    c. Begin process to enhance curriculum to maximize opportunities for students to earn college credits through dual credit classes and AP classes that mandate the AP test itself.

WEEK TWO:

1. Principals, Superintendent, and School Board:

   a. Introduce the new Mission to all K-12 staff, advocating for and explaining why "We Create Two- and Four-Year College Graduates with Minimal Debt." Lay out your version of the plan for implementation (described below).

   b. Get buy-in from staff. Receive input from staff on the implementation plan.

   c. Have counselors speak about how they will help educate all staff so that all teachers can be assistant college counselors, serving the new Mission—for their students and their own children.

2. Teachers: Set up faculty groups to ensure everyone has a role.

   a. Messaging Committee: entrusted with deciding what messages will go up on new banners and where, and on TV screens in schools.

   b. Summer Committee(s): entrusted with fighting the summer slide through advocacy for affordable, local, productive summer opportunities. Faculty within each high school department—Math, English, Science, Social Studies, the Arts, etc.—convene to amplify the Mission within their rooms. The leaders of each department get together at least quarterly to share the summer programs that each department is promoting to their students. At smaller schools, faculty across all disciplines can work in a single group on summer advocacy.

c. The faculty from each department will develop a list of all worthy, affordable and pricey, discipline-related summer opportunities available to students within 75 miles—and perhaps beyond. The English teachers will put together a list of writing, literature, theater, grammar, Shakespeare, and other English related camps and activities. The science department will do the same for science camps and activities, etc…

d. Learn about and promote some camps nationally as well. For example, many camps nationally seek minorities and offer very low-cost experiences. Ensure that your minority students learn about them.

e. Each department will then put together specifics regarding these camps—costs, application dates, scholarship information, contact info, any editorial thoughts about the camps (rank them perhaps based on value and quality)—and post them on line and on their walls. Teachers can split up the list, research and summarize the publicized details about each, and also contact camp leaders. That personal contact can help ensure that your school's students get in for less.

f. Each teacher can then promote camps on the list that have an approaching application deadline, helping and encouraging students to attend.

3. Counselors:

a. Empower your counseling department to assemble all relevant scholarship, cost, deadline, and other germane information regarding the favorite, nearby colleges of your seniors.

b. Counselors might assemble similar information for their favorite farther-away colleges: engineering, most affordable, etc. JBP's *College Common Sense: Get into Your Best Fit College & Spend Less* and *JBP's College Common Sense: America's Most Affordable Colleges* can help.

c. Counselors are the point people for turning the entire staff into informed assistant college counselors and all students into knowledgeable applicants capable of finding their perfect fit colleges without overspending or over borrowing.

Week three:

1. Principals and Superintendent:

   a. Communicate the new Mission privately to parent leaders, community leaders, and boosters, explaining why it's crucial and how you're rolling it out.

   b. Enhance curriculum to maximize opportunities for students to earn college credits through dual credit classes and AP classes that mandate the AP test itself.

2. Teachers:

   a. Messaging Committee
      Finalize all messages. Possibilities include:

      - #1) No College Degree, #2) A College Degree with Excessive Debt, or #3) A College Degree with Minimal Debt. Choose #3!

      - Only Wimps Pay Full Price for College.

      - We expect everyone here to be a two- or four-year college graduate with minimal debt by age 24.

      - Everyone here can be a two- or four-year college graduate with minimal debt by age 24.

      - Get an education, not just a degree.

      - Slackers Rarely Get Scholarships

      - School is Your Economic Trampoline. Get a two- or four-year College Degree with Minimal Debt by age 24.

- School is Your Economic Launching Pad. Get a two- or four-year College Degree with Minimal Debt by age 24.

- Hammer the Grammar

- Welders and Diesel Mechanics can make $30,000 to $55,000 a year by age 22.

- Join the 55 percent! Start and finish college within four years!

- Arm Yourself to Compete Against Intelligent Machines and Low-Cost Foreign Labor: Get a Two- or Four-Year College Degree With Minimal (or NO) Debt!

- Arm Yourself to Compete: Get a Two- or Four-Year College Degree With Minimal (or NO) Debt!

- A Proven Pathway to The Skills and Knowledge You'll Need to Compete: a Two- or Four-Year College Degree with Minimal (or NO) Debt!

 i. Have students create the signs. Or order them at www.JohnBaylorPrep.com. This should be your primary financial cost of rolling out your new Mission.

b. Summer Committee(s)

Keep assembling information on summer enrichment opportunities so that they can be finalized and ready by Week Six.

3. Counselors:

   a. Finish assembling your bullet point info regarding favorite nearby colleges.

   b. Decide what topics will make for helpful four-minute videos for email blasts and the school's web site. With so many students per counselor, communicating the Mission effectively via technology is critical. Possible video topics include:

   - How ROTC works.

   - Retail Sticker Price vs. Net Cost—why our grads shouldn't expect to pay retail sticker

   - Our state's Flagship Public University: retail sticker price, typical net costs, scholarships, and how to apply.

   - Our state's non-Flagship Public Universities: sticker prices, typical net costs, scholarships, and how to apply.

   - Nearby private colleges: sticker price, typical net costs, scholarships, and how to apply.

   - How you can and why you should become a college graduate with minimal debt.

   - Mistakes made by past applicants.

   - What middle school students should know and do about getting into the best fit college at the lowest cost.

- What ninth, tenth, eleventh and twelfth grade students should know and do about getting into the best fit college at the lowest cost.

- Helpful services for first generation minority and lower income college applicants (QuestBridge, Susan Buffet Foundation, etc.)

Create a video club of students who will videotape you in these videos and then edit them. Video Club will be a valuable extracurricular on their future college applications.

WEEK FOUR:

1. Principals and Superintendent:

    a. Letter out to families explaining the Mission, why it's important, and how it will be executed and measured using the National Clearinghouse for two- and four-year graduation percentages.

    b. Ask counselors to plan for and take 30 minutes at a future staff meeting to educate all staff on key details of how students can get into their Best Fit college at the lowest cost.

    c. With counselors, implement a plan to have juniors take the ACT or SAT twice and seniors to take either twice, preparing juniors during school for the February or April ACT and seniors during school for the September or October ACT.

    d. Encourage all sophomores with a chance at winning a national merit scholarship (on their junior year, October PSAT), to prepare for and take the June sophomore year ACT.

2. Teachers:

    a. Messaging Committee
        i. Finalize all messages.
        ii. Have students create the banners, or order them at www.JohnBaylorPrep.com.

    b. Summer Committee(s)
        i. Keep assembling information on summer enrichment opportunities so that they can be finalized and ready by Week Six.

3. Counselors:

    a. Get pennants from each college attended by last year's senior class. (This may be another minor expense, though many college admissions offices, if asked, will send you a pennant and other gear for free.)

    b. Get the video club started, recruiting student members.

    c. Write, shoot, and post four-minute counseling videos for web site and email blasts.

    d. Finish assembling your bullet point info regarding favorite nearby colleges.

WEEK FIVE:

1. Principals and Superintendents:

   a. Full School Meeting with Students, explaining the Mission—why it's critical and how counselors and staff will help it happen. Show the JBP public vignette *Become a Two- or Four-Year College Grad with Minimal Debt.* (14 minutes, no cost)

   b. The day of your all-school meeting, blast an email to parents to reinforce the Mission. For example, you might blast to all your families the JBP public vignette *Become a Two- or Four-Year College Grad with Minimal Debt.* Thus, parents and students now will have all the same information explaining why and how. Healthy conversations should occur at many homes.

   c. Ask counselors to take five minutes to update staff on the latest scholarship, college costs, application dates, FAFSA information, and any other college related developments at most future staff meetings—whether weekly, bimonthly, or monthly.

2. Teachers:

   a. Hang your diploma in your room.

   b. Messaging Committee
      i. Finalize all messages.
      ii. Have students create the banners—or order them at www.JohnBaylorPrep.com.

   c. Summer Committee(s)
      Keep assembling information on summer enrichment opportunities so that they can be finalized and ready by Week Six.

3. Counselors:

    a.   Prepare to present to faculty so that they can be assistant college counselors, armed with the basics regarding how to get into popular nearby colleges for less. For example, specifics on scholarships, deadlines, and academic strengths of the 8-10 most popular college destinations for your students. Explain that all students will be encouraged to apply to at least seven colleges, including at least two financial safety schools within their family's budget, and to take the ACT four times. All students will be encouraged to have the "Money Talk" with parents by sophomore year.

    b.   Prepare to update faculty for five minutes at future staff meetings.

    c.   Write, shoot, and post four-minute counseling videos for web site and email blasts.

    d.   Help Summer Committee(s) finalize their lists of summer programming to promote.

WEEK SIX:

1. Principals and Superintendent:

   a. Full evening meeting with parents to explain the new Mission: why and how.

   b. Contact and explain the new Mission to local media.

   c. Communicate now and regularly with thriving local businesses to ensure that your Mission and curriculum teach the skills they seek.

2. Teachers:

   a. Messaging Committee
      i. Finalize all banners and signs.
      ii. Have students create them.

   b. Summer Committee(s)
      i. Keep assembling information on summer enrichment opportunities.
      ii. Ensure that the counseling office has a growing master list of all summer programs the staff is promoting.
      iii. Begin promoting your summer programs to all your students. Fight the summer slide.

3. Counselors:

   a. Prepare to update faculty for five minutes at each future staff meeting. In the counseling office have an ever-growing master list of summer programs to promote.

   b. Keep collecting pennants from colleges attended by last year's senior class. Hang the pennants. List the name(s) of each member of last year's senior class underneath the pennant representing his current college. Others go under a "straight to job market" or "straight to military" home-made pennant.

c. Hang a sign in your office with the percentage of graduates each of the last three years attending a four-year college, a two-year college, and no college. Update this sign each August.

d. Once informed by the National Clearinghouse, hang a sign with each graduating year's two- and four-year college graduation rate, starting with your graduation class from six years ago and going backwards.

Week seven:

1. Principals and Superintendent:

   a. Ensure all staff can give the two-minute explanation for the Mission—the why and the how—to any student, parent, or community member.

   b. Ensure there is strong Mission messaging in the elementary and middle schools (banners, signs, etc.).

2. Teachers:

   a. Messaging Committee

      i. Finalize all and hang all banners and messages.

      ii. Ensure that all faculty can convey the two-minute explanation, using similar language.

   b. Summer Committee(s)

      i. Keep assembling information on and promoting summer enrichment opportunities.

      ii. Ensure that the counseling office has a growing master list of all summer programs the staff is promoting.

   c. All

      i. Regularly share the Mission of why graduation with minimal debt matters and how to get there.

3. Counselors:

   a. In the counseling office have an ever-growing master list of summer programs to promote.

   b. Post pennants from colleges attended by last year's senior class. List the names of each student at that college underneath its pennant.

c. Keep creating four-minute videos on important college admissions related information. Post these videos on the school's website, email them to parents, and text them to students.

WEEK EIGHT:

1. Principals and Superintendent:

    a. Ongoing: Keep selling parents and community leaders on the *Reaching Higher* Mission as a means to improve your students' future prospects, as well as your community's.

2. Teachers:

    a. Messaging Committee
        i. Finalize all visible banners and messages.
    b. Summer Committee(s)
        i. Keep assembling information on and promoting summer enrichment opportunities.
        ii. Ensure that the counseling office has a growing master list of all summer programs the staff is promoting.

3. Counselors:

    a. Ongoing: Regularly update faculty on scholarship, retail sticker price, and all other college cost and quality related issues.
    b. Ongoing: In the counseling office have an ever-growing master list of summer programs to promote.
    c. Ongoing: Keep creating four-minute videos on important college admissions related information. Post these videos on the school's website, email them to parents, and text them to students.

QUARTERLY

Every quarter thereafter, discuss how the Mission and message is becoming central to the culture—your school district's core value effectively. Discuss how it can be reinforced further through technology, quick speeches at large parent gatherings, new signage, new testimonials from past graduates, stronger messaging in the elementary and middle schools, etc.

ANNUALLY

The Mission will need to be refreshed at least annually as new teachers and students arrive, and they seek the latest information on local college costs and scholarships, the job skills most in demand locally, what those skills pay, the most affordable four-year colleges nationally, etc.

LOOKING FORWARD

Once inculcated into your culture within eight weeks, there's no reason the Mission should ever dissipate. It can be part of your school's DNA. With minimal additional effort, your current and future Kindergarten through twelfth grade students should receive this expectation organically, along with the blueprint for how to get there.

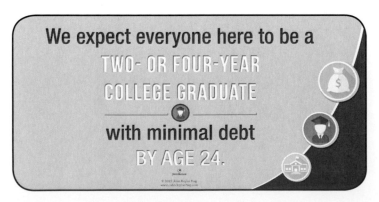

ACKNOWLEDGMENTS

Thank you Lauren Glett and Ali Roth for your research, footnotes, and bibliography. Thank you Deb Selby for taking care of so much JBP work so that I could devote more time to *Reaching Higher*.

Thank you to the many who scrutinized earlier drafts and gave me needed critiques. These include Ken Kiewra, John Dewey, Colleen McCoy, Perry Herman, Joni Woodruff, Celeste Fortenberry, Jeff Fortenberry, John Skretta, Dan Alberts, Dan Bertrand, Pat Combs, Ed Renwick, Scott Shepard, and many others.

Thank you to the many who agreed to be interviewed for this book. Your input has greatly enriched it.

Thanks to my publisher, Lisa Pelto and the staff at Concierge Marketing Publishing Services, for coming up with the title and shepherding this effort.

Thank you to the thousands of students I've taught. Your reactions are the lessons that fill these pages.

Thank you to the more than 350 high schools using JBP to strengthen their scores, scholarships, and culture. Your reactions to my presentations covering the *Reaching Higher* theme have refined the Mission and strengthened my belief in its power to transform K-12 education.

Thank you to my wife Susan, who tolerates my odd hours and makes sure our children always know they're loved, despite a too often absent, working father. And thank you to our children, Sophia, Chloe, Antonia, and Cameron, who exude a love for learning every day. Their questions, passions, and laughter push me to be worthy of them.

ABOUT THE AUTHOR

John Baylor is the founder and owner of John Baylor Prep, which helps schools and families create two and four-year college graduates with minimal debt. John has taught tens of thousands of students over more than two decades. He and JBP work with more than 350 high schools nationwide, improving motivation, school cultures, and test scores. John also has been a play-by-play sportscaster for more than twenty years. He lives with his wife and children in Lincoln, Nebraska.

ENDNOTES

1. Citizen Schools. 2007. Fast Company. 3 January 2014 <http://www.fastcompany.com/social/2007/profiles/profile7.html>.

2. Crotty, James Marshall. "Motivation Matters: 40% Of High School Students Chronically Disengaged From School." 13 March 2013. Forbes. 26 May 2014

3. Busteed, Brandon. "The School Cliff: Student Engagement Drops With Each School Year." 7 January 2013. Gallup Blog. 26 May 2014 <http://thegallupblog.gallup.com/2013/01/the-school-cliff-student-engagement.html>

4. Clausing, Jeri. "Gates Says Fixing Education Toughest Challenge." 1 July 2014. Huffington Post. 22 July 2014 <http://www.huffingtonpost.com/2014/07/01/bill-gates-education-challenge_n_5547848.html>.

5. Pope, Denise Clark. "Doing School: How We Are Creating a Generation of Stressed-Out, Materialistic, and Miseducated Students." Yale University Press, 2003.

6. Deresiewicz, William. Excellent Sheep. Free Press, 2014.

7. Ingraham, Christopher. "10 maps that show how much time Americans spend grooming, eating, thinking and praying." 20 June 2014. Washington Post. 14 July 2014 <http://www.washingtonpost.com/blogs/wonkblog/wp/2014/06/20/ten-maps-that-show-how-much-time-americans-spend-grooming-eating-thinking-and-praying/>.

8. Graham, Ian. "Television viewing: Countries Compared." 2002. Nation Master. 22 July 2014 <http://www.nationmaster.com/country-info/stats/Media/Television-viewing>.

9. Herr, Norman. "Television & Health ." 2007. California State University. 22 July 2014 <http://www.csun.edu/science/health/docs/tv&health.html>.

10. Riggs, Liz. "Why Do Teachers Quit?" 18 October 2013. The Atlantic. 3 January 2015 <http://www.theatlantic.com/education/archive/2013/10/why-do-teachers-quit/280699/2/) >.

11. US Census Bureau. 2013. 3 January 2015 <http://www.census.gov/hhes/socdemo/education/data/cps/historical/fig11.jpg >.

12. Korkki, Phyllis. "The Ripple Effects of Rising Student Debt." 24 May 2014. New York Times. 26 May 2014 <http://www.nytimes.com/2014/05/25/business/the-ripple-effects-of-rising-student-debt.html?_r=0>.

13. Aldeman, Chad. "Great News: Fewer Students Attending High School Dropout Factories" 2015. Ahead of the Heard Blog. 27 May 2015. http://aheadoftheheard.org/great-news-fewer-students-attending-high-school-dropout-factories/.

14. MissionStatements.Com. "School Mission Statements." 2014. 2 June 2014 <http://www.missionstatements.com/school_Mission_statements.html>.

15. Ibid.

16. Starbucks. "Our Starbucks Mission Statement ." 2014. 2 June 2014 <http://www.starbucks.com/about-us/company-information/Mission-statement>.

17. McCormack, Richard A. "It Will Be A Long Time Before Chinese Manufacturing Wages Catch Up With American's: China's Hourly Manufacturing Worker Compensation Cost: $1.74." 17 June 2013. Manufacturing and Technology News. 22 July 2014 <http://www.manufacturingnews.com/news/chinawages0617131.html>.

18. Bradsher, Keith and Duhigg Charles. "How the US Lost Out on iPhone Work." 21 January 2012. New York Times. 3 January 2015 <http://www.nytimes.com/2012/01/22/business/apple-america-and-a-squeezed-middle-class.html>.

19. ICEF Monitor. "China and India to Produce 40% of Global Graduates by 2020." 16 July 2012. ICEF Monitor. 26 May 2014 <http://monitor.icef.com/2012/07/china-and-india-to-produce-40-of-global-graduates-by-2020/>.

20. Farmers Edge. "Neat Facts About United States Agriculture." 4 July 2013. 14 July 2014 <http://www.farmersedge.ca/blog/2013/07/04/neat-facts-about-united-states-agriculture>.

21. Bureau of Labor Statistics. "Employment Projections." December 2013. 14 July 2014 <http://www.bls.gov/emp/ep_table_201.htm>.

22. United States Department of Agriculture. "Fact Book." 03 January 2015 <http://www.usda.gov/factbook/chapter2.pdf>.

23. Herbert, Bob. Losing Our Way. 2014.

24. Boyd Meyers, Courtney. "The Humanoids Are Here." 22 June 2009. Forbes. 26 May 2014 <http://www.forbes.com/2009/06/18/humanoid-robots-asimo-opinions-contributor-artificial-intelligence-09-myers.html>.

25. Aquino, Judith. "Nine Jobs that Humans May Lose to Robots ." 2012. NBC News. 26 May 2014 <http://www.nbcnews.com/id/42183592/ns/business-careers/t/nine-jobs-humans-may-lose-robots/#.U4OaKpRdVjI>.

26. Summers, Lawrence. "Lawrence H. Summers on the Economic Challenge of the Future: Jobs." 7 July 2014. Wall Street Journal. 22 July 2014 <http://online.wsj.com/articles/lawrence-h-summers-on-the-economic-challenge-of-the-future-jobs-1404762501>.

27. The Economist. "Coming to an office near you." 18 January 2014. 3 January 2015 <http://www.economist.com/news/leaders/21594298-effect-todays-technology-tomorrows-jobs-will-be-immenseand-no-country-ready>.

28. Hanson, Robin. "The Economics of Brain Emulations ." 26 May 2014 <http://hanson.gmu.edu/EconOfBrainEmulations.pdf>.

29. The Examiner. "Technology Doesn't Improve Education. Teachers Do. ." 10 April 2012. 14 July 2014 <http://www.examiner.com/article/technology-doesn-t-improve-education-teachers-do>.

30. United States Census Bureau. "Educational Attainment." 2013. 14 July 2014 <http://www.census.gov/hhes/socdemo/education/data/cps/2013/tables.html>.

31. Levy, F. and R.J. Murnane. "The new division of labor: How computers are creating the next job market." Princeton University Press, 2004.

32. Frey, Carl Benedikt and Michael A. Osborne. "The Future of Employment: How Susceptible Are Jobs to Computerisation?" 17 September 2013. 3 January 2015 <http://www.oxfordmartin.ox.ac.uk/downloads/academic/The_Future_of_Employment.pdf>.

33. Cowen, Tyler. *Average Is Over: Powering America Beyond the Age of the Great Stagnation.* Dutton Adult, 2013.

34. Carr, Austin. "Report: Apps to explode to $38 billion market by 2015." 1 March 2011. CNN Tech. 26 May 2014 <http://www.cnn.com/2011/TECH/mobile/03/01/app.growth.tech/index.html>.

35. Plumer, Brad. "How the recession turned middle-class jobs into low-wage jobs." 28 February 2013. Washington Post. 26 May 2014 <http://www.washingtonpost.com/blogs/wonkblog/wp/2013/02/28/how-the-recession-turned-middle-class-jobs-into-low-wage-jobs/>.

36. Ibid.

37. Becker, Gary. "Concern About The Decline in Manufacturing in the United States?" 2011. The Becker-Posner Blog. 30 April 2012. <http://www.becker-posner-blog.com/2012/04/concern-about-the-decline-in-manufacturing-in-the-united-states-becker.html>.

38. Tankersley, Jim. "The Devalued American Worker ." 21 December 2014. Washington Post. 22 January 2015 <http://www.washingtonpost.com/sf/business/2014/12/14/the-devalued-american-worker/>.

39. Synder, Michael. "No Jobs, No Hope, No Future: 27 Signs That America's Poverty Class Is Rapidly Becoming Larger Than America's Middle Class." 25 January 2011. The American Dream. 25 July 2014 <http://endoftheamericandream.com/archives/no-jobs-no-hope-no-future-27-signs-that-americas-poverty-class-is-rapidly-becoming-larger-than-americas-middle-class>.

40. Cowen, Tyler. *Average Is Over: Powering America Beyond the Age of the Great Stagnation.* Dutton Adult, 2013.

41. Ibid, Pg. 3.

42. Guynn, Jessica. "How Instagram founder Kevin Systrom became insta-rich." 11 April 2012. Los Angeles Times. 26 May 2014 <http://articles.latimes.com/2012/apr/11/business/la-fi-instagram-systrom-20120411>.Zewali, Ahmed. "2011 Commencement Speech ." 2011. Caltech Commencement. 3 January 2015 <https://commencement.caltech.edu/archive/speakers/2011_address>.

43. Peters, Mark and David Wessel. "More Men in Prime Working Ages Don't Have Jobs." 6 February 2014. Wall Street Journal. 14 July 2014 <http://online.wsj.com/news/articles/SB10001424052702304027204579334610097660366>.

44. NET. "The State Of Education In Nebraska: The Future Of Education." 17 July 2014. 25 July 2014 <http://netnebraska.org/interactive-multimedia/learning-services/state-education-nebraska-future-education-118>.

45. Weddle, DJ. John Baylor Prep. 3 January 2015 <http://www.johnbaylorprep.com/jbp-testimonials/schools>.

46. Krause, Heather. "Guess Who Cares For Young Adults When They Move Home ." 5 May 2014. FiveThirtyEightLife. 2 June 2014 <http://fivethirtyeight.com/features/guess-who-cares-for-young-adults-when-they-move-back-home/#print>.

47. Korkki, Phyllis. "The Ripple Effects of Rising Student Debt." 24 May 2014. New York Times. 26 May 2014 <http://www.nytimes.com/2014/05/25/business/the-ripple-effects-of-rising-student-debt.html?_r=0>.

48. Rocheleau, Matt. "College costs top inflation, even with financial aid." 22 June 2014. Boston Globe. 14 July 2014 <http://www.bostonglobe.com/metro/2014/06/21/net-prices-mass-private-colleges-rise-sharply-despite-increase-financial-aid/ccvqO49scwRvd4uIfsXz3H/story.html>.

49. Rossi, Andrew. "Is College Worth the Cost? ." 19 November 2014. CNN. 3 January 2015 <http://www.cnn.com/2014/11/19/opinion/ivory-tower-andrew-rossi-higher-education-cost/index.html>.

50. Ibid.

51. Ibid.

52. American Student Assistance. "Life Delayed: The Impact of Student Debt on the Daily Lives of Young Americans." 2013. 25 May 2014 <http://www.asa.org/pdfs/corporate/life-delayed.pdf>.

53. The Wall Street Journal. 25 May 2014 <http://online.wsj.com/news/articles/SB10001424052970204731804574388682129316614?mg=reno64-wsj&url=http%3A%2F%2Fonline.wsj.com%2Farticle%2FSB10001424052970204731804574388682129316614.html>.

54. Ingraham, Christopher. "Most college students literally have no idea how much they're paying to go to school." 11 December 2014. Washington Post. 22 January 2015

55. Leonhardt, David. "Is College Worth It? Clearly, New Data Say." 27 May 2014. New York Times. 25 July 2014 <http://www.nytimes.com/2014/05/27/upshot/is-college-worth-it-clearly-new-data-say.html?_r=1>

56. Associated Press. "Graduates earn $1M more over a lifetime." 25 June 2014. The Daily Star. 14 July 2014 <http://www.dailystar.com.lb/Business/International/2014/Jun-25/261450-graduates-earn-1m-more-over-a-lifetime.ashx#axzz37VH4sKAE>.

57. Tough, Paul. "Who Gets to Graduate?" 15 May 2014. New York Times. 2 June 2014 <http://nyti.ms/1gqD4Wa>.

58. Fisher, Daniel. "Poor Students Are The Real Victims Of College Discrimination." 2 May 2012. 15 July 2014 <http://www.forbes.com/sites/danielfisher/2012/05/02/poor-students-are-the-real-victims-of-college-discrimination/>.

59. NYT, David Brooks, May 1, 2015: "The Nature of Poverty."

60. Ibid.

61. National Center for Education Statistics. "Public School Students Eligible for Free or Reduced-Price Lunch." 2009. 3 January 2015 <http://nces.ed.gov/programs/digest/d09/tables/dt09_042.asp>.

62. Ibid.

63. Seidel, Aly and Claire Trageser. "Coaching First-Generation Students Through College." 3 July 2014. NprEd. 15 July 2014 <http://www.npr.org/blogs/ed/2014/07/03/327253265/coaching-first-generation-students-through-college>.

64. NPR Staff. "How One Michigan City Is Sending Kids To College Tuition-Free." 16 April 2014. NPR. 14 July 2014 <http://www.npr.org/2014/04/16/303365867/how-one-michigan-city-is-sending-kids-to-college-tuition-free>.

65. W.E. Upjohn Institute. 15 July 2014 <http://www.upjohn.org/>.

66. NPR Staff. "How One Michigan City Is Sending Kids To College Tuition-Free." 16 April 2014. NPR. 14 July 2014 <http://www.npr.org/2014/04/16/303365867/how-one-michigan-city-is-sending-kids-to-college-tuition-free>.

67. Tough, Paul. "Who Gets to Graduate?" 15 May 2014. New York Times. 15 July 2014 <http://nyti.ms/1gqD4Wa>.

68. Ibid.

69. Turner, Cory and Claudio Sanchez. "College For Free: Tulsa's Radical Idea." 11 June 2014. NPR. 14 July 2014 <http://www.npr.org/blogs/ed/2014/06/11/320633113/college-for-free-tulsa-radical-idea>.

70. Paulson, Amanda. "Inner-city Chicago charter school has perfect college acceptance rate." 8 April 2010. Christian Science Monitor. 27 May 2014 <http://www.csmonitor.com/USA/Society/2010/0408/Inner-city-Chicago-charter-school-has-perfect-college-acceptance-rate>.

71. Ibid.

72. Perez-Pena, Richard. "New York Times." 25 October 2013. Despite Rising Sticker Prices, Actual College Costs Stable Over Decade, Study Says. 3 January 2015 <http://www.nytimes.com/2013/10/25/education/despite-rising-sticker-prices-actual-college-costs-stable-over-decade-study-says.html>.

73. Krugman, Paul. "Degrees and Dollars." 7 March 2011. <http://www.nytimes.com/2011/03/07/opinion/07krugman.html>.https://cew.georgetown.edu/wp-content/uploads/2014/11/Recovery2020.ES_.Web_.pdf

74. Carnevale, Anthony and Smith, Nicole and Strohl, Jeff. 2014. Recovery: Job Growth and Education Requirements through 2020. p.1, Executive Summary. Georgetown Public Policy Institute: Center on Education and the Workforce. <https://cew.georgetown.edu/wp-content/uploads/2014/11/Recovery2020.ES_.Web_.pdf>.

75. The Do School. 26 May 2014 <The Do School>.

76. Enstitute. 26 May 2014 <http://www.enstituteu.com/>.

77. Tompor, Susan. "Will you marry me (and my student loan debt)?" 25 May 2013. USA Today. 26 May 2014 <http://www.usatoday.com/story/money/columnist/2013/05/25/student-debt-marriage-wedding-loans/2351405/>.

78. Wright, Peggy. "High school senior suing parents for college tuition ." 3 March 2014. USA Today. 26 May 2014 <http://www.usatoday.com/story/news/nation/2014/03/03/student-sues-parents-college-tuition/5967279/>.

79. Reynolds, Glenn Harlan. "Higher ed becoming a joke." 19 May 2014. USA Today. 26 May 2014 <http://www.usatoday.com/story/opinion/2014/05/19/college-graduation-rice-lagarde-higher-education-costs-tuition-column/9249371/>.

80. Sheehy, Kelsey. "10 Colleges Where Grads Have the Most Student Loan Debt." 17 December 2013. US News. 27 May 2014 <http://www.usnews.com/education/best-colleges/the-short-list-college/articles/2013/12/17/10-colleges-where-grads-have-the-most-student-loan-debt>.

81. Ivory Tower. By Andrew Rossi. Dirs. Darin Farriola and Andrew Rossi. 2014.

82. Ibid.

83. Ibid.

84. Leonhardt, David. "Is College Worth It? Clearly, New Data Say ." 27 May 2014. New York Times. 25 July 2014 <http://www.nytimes.com/2014/05/27/upshot/is-college-worth-it-clearly-new-data-say.html?_r=1>

85. Autor, David. "Skills, education, and the rise of earnings inequality among the (other 99 percent)." 23 May 2014. Science. 14 July 2014 <http://www.sciencemag.org/content/344/6186/843>.

86. Ivory Tower. By Andrew Rossi. Dirs. Darin Farriola and Andrew Rossi. 2014.

87. Gentile, Douglas. "Pathological Video Game Use among Youth 8 to 18: A National Study." 20 April 2009. Iowa State University News. 27 May 2014 <http://www.public.iastate.edu/~nscentral/news/2009/apr/vgaddiction.shtml>.

88. National Center for Education Statistics. "Projections of Education Statistics to 2021." January 2013. Institute of Education Sciences. 27 May 2014 <http://nces.ed.gov/programs/projections/projections2021/tables/table_12.asp>.

89. Leonhardt, David. "Bill Gates, College Dropout: Don't Be Like Me" 3 June 15. <http://www.nytimes.com/2015/06/04/upshot/bill-gates-college-dropout-dont-be-like-me.html?_r=0&abt=0002&abg=1>.

90. Wagner, Eric. "Five Reasons 8 Out Of 10 Businesses Fail." 12 September 2013. Forbes. 25 July 2014 <http://www.forbes.com/sites/ericwagner/2013/09/12/five-reasons-8-out-of-10-businesses-fail/>.

91. Jacoby, Tamar. "This Way Up: Mobility in America." 22 July 2014. Wall Street Journal. 3 January 2015 <http://www.wsj.com/articles/this-way-up-mobility-in-america-1405710779>.

92. O'Neill, Lauren. "Robots could soon replace fast food workers, study says." 28 May 2014. CBC News. 3 January 2015 <http://www.cbc.ca/newsblogs/yourcommunity/2014/05/robots-could-soon-replace-fast-food-workers-study-says.html>.

93. Beauty Schools Directory. "Cosmetology School Cost, Tuition & Financial Aid." 14 July 2014 <http://www.beautyschoolsdirectory.com/metrosearch.php>.

94. Army ROTC. "Service Commitment." 14 July 2014 <http://www.goarmy.com/rotc/service-commitment.html>.

95. Woods, Laura. 20 January 2015. Go Banking Rates. 22 January 2015 <Gobankingrates.com>.

96. Lu, Adrienne. "States Crack Down on For-Profit Colleges, Student Loan Industry." 14 April 2014. The Pew Charitable Trusts. 15 July 2014 <http://www.pewtrusts.org/en/research-and-analysis/blogs/stateline/2014/04/14/states-crack-down-on-forprofit-colleges-student-loan-industry>.

97. Vinik, Danny. "Obama Is Cracking Down on For-Profit Colleges—And Liberals Should Applaud Him for It." 17 March 2014. New Republic. 15 July 2014 <http://www.newrepublic.com/article/117049/white-house-issues-gainful-employment-regulation-profit-colleges>.

98. Mitchell, Josh. "Defaults on Federal Student Loans Decline." 25 September 2014. Wall Street Journal. 3 January 2015 <http://www.wsj.com/articles/defaults-on-federal-student-loans-decline-1411567201>.

99. Perez-Pena, Richard. "College Group Run for Profit Looks to Close or Sell Schools." 4 July 2014. New York Times. 15 July 2014 <http://www.nytimes.com/2014/07/05/education/corinthian-colleges-to-largely-shut-down.html?emc=edit_th_20140705&nl=todaysheadlines&nlid=37310502&_r=0>.

100. State of California Department of Justice. "Attorney General Kamala D. Harris Files Suit in Alleged For-Profit College Predatory Scheme." 10 October 2013. 15 July 2014 <http://oag. ca.gov/news/press-releases/attorney-general-kamala-d-harris-files-suit-alleged-profit-college-predatory>.

101. O'Shaughnessy, Lynn. "The Odds of Getting an Athletic Scholarship." 10 May 2012. The College Solution. 3 January 2015 <http://www.thecollegesolution.com/the-odds-of-getting-an-athletic-scholarship-2/ >.

102. NprEd. "Tough Lessons On Debt For College Students." 2 May 2014. 14 July 2014 <http://www.npr.org/blogs/ed/2014/05/02/308950755/tough-lessons-on-debt-for-college-students>.

103. Anderson, Nick. "Students encouraged to apply to college, while in class." 20 December 2014. Washington Post. 3 January 2015 <http://www.beaumontenterprise.com/news/article/Students-encouraged-to-apply-to-college-while-in-59/0465.php>.

104. *University of Nebraska Cornhuskers Pennant NCAA.* Digital Image. *Team Fanatics.* Web. 3 January 2015 <http:// http://teamfanatics.com/products/university-of-nebraska-cornhuskers-pennant-ncaa?utm_source=googleshopping&utm_medium=cse&gclid=CLTR2KLj4L8CFUKCMgodlA8AFA>/

105. *Creighton Bluejays Premium Pennant.* Digital Image. *Amazon Prime.* Web. 3 January 2015 <http://www.amazon.com/Hall-of-Fame-Memorabilia-Creighton/dp/B00KB4N82W>.

106. *University of Nebraska-Kearney Lopers 6 X 15 Flocked Pennant.* Digital Image. *Neebo.* Web. 3 January 2015 < http://www.neebo.com/Shop/flags-pennants/university-of-nebraskakearney-antelopes-6-x-15-flocked-pennant>.

107. *Chadron State Eagles 12 X 30 One Piece Color Pennant.* Digital Image. *Neebo.* Web. 3 January 2015 <http://www.neebo.com/Shop/house-home-accessories/chadron-state-college-eagles-12-x-30-one-piece-color-pennantg2700902>.

108. Jacoby, Tamar. "This Way Up: Mobility in America." 22 July 2014. Wall Street Journal. 3 January 2015 <http://www.wsj.com/articles/this-way-up-mobility-in-america-1405710779>.

109. Byrd, Alan and Williams, Allison. "Role for everyone to keep high school graduates on college path." 4 June 2015. <http://www.stltoday.com/news/opinion/columns/role-for-everyone-to-keep-high-school-graduates-on-college/article_54c341ef-4e4f-58a3-a6e9-5694a7a495ff.html?mobile_touch=true>.

110. National Student Clearinghouse. "StudentTracker for High Schools." 15 July 2014 <http://www.studentclearinghouse.org/high_schools/studenttracker/>.

111. Leonhardt, David. "Bill Gates, College Dropout: Don't Be Like Me" 3 June 15. <http://www.nytimes.com/2015/06/04/upshot/bill-gates-college-dropout-dont-be-like-me.html?_r=0&abt=0002&abg=1>.

112. Ivory Tower. By Andrew Rossi. Dirs. Darin Farriola and Andrew Rossi. 2014.

113. Ibid.

114. Arum, Richard and Josipa Roksa. Academically Adrift. Chicago: University Of Chicago Press, 2010.

115. Association of American Colleges and Universities. "New Report Documents That Liberal Arts Disciplines Prepare Graduates for Long-Term Professional Success." 22 January 2014. 14 July 2014 <http://www.aacu.org/press_room/press_releases/2014/liberalartsreport.cfmA>.

116. King, Tracey and Bannon, Ellynne. "At What Cost? The Price That Working Students Pay For A College Education ." April 2002. 15 July 2014 <http://www.pirg.org/highered/atwhatcost4_16_02.pdf>.

117. National Conference of State Legislators. "Hot Topics in Higher Education Reforming Remedial Education ." 2011. 3 January 2015 <http://www.ncsl.org/research/education/improving-college-completion-reforming-remedial.aspx>.

118. Ibid.

119. Ibid.

120. Ibid.

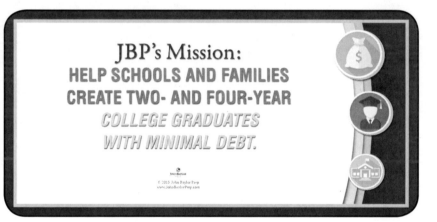